A Blindfold Removed

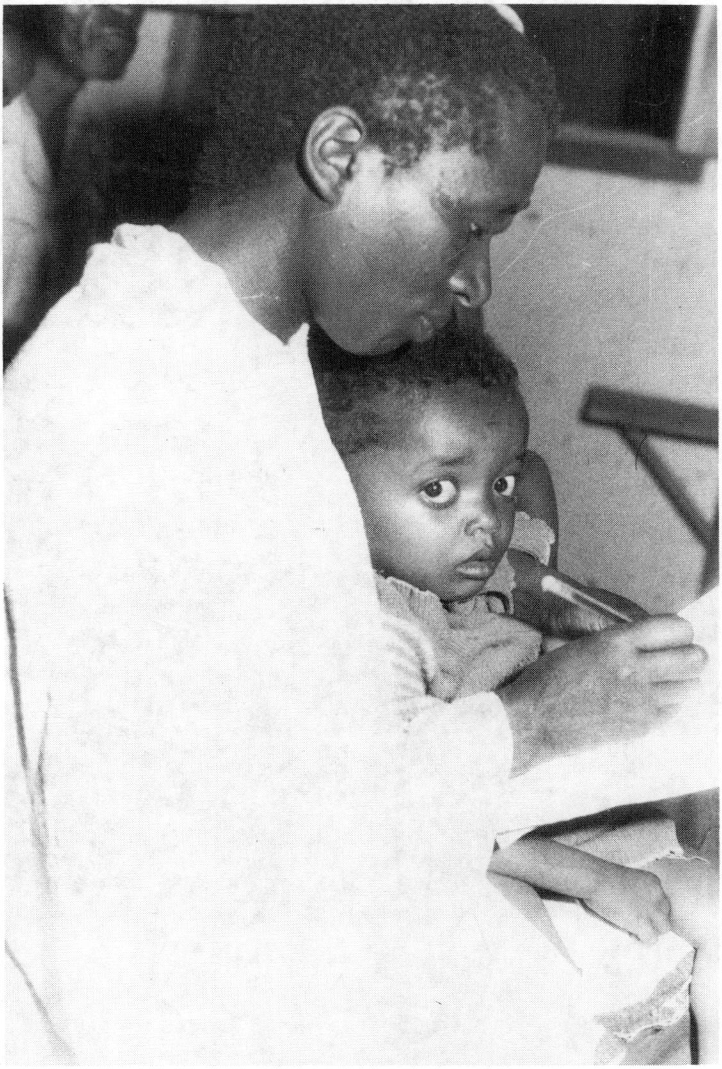

A BLINDFOLD REMOVED: ETHIOPIA'S STRUGGLE FOR LITERACY

by
Chris Searle

KARIA PRESS

YOUNG WORLD BOOKS

A BLINDFOLD REMOVED:
Ethiopia's Struggle For Literacy

First published in 1991 by **Karia Press**
and **Young World Books**

Typeset by **Karia Communications**

Photographs: Getachew Awoke and the National Literacy Campaign of Ethiopia

ISBN 1 85465 008 4 Pb

Karia Press, 41 Rheola Close, London N17 9TR
Young World Books, 490 Kingsland Road, London E8

Printed and bound in Great Britain by
Biddles Ltd, Guildford and King's Lynn

Contents

About the Author 7

Glossary 7

ACKNOWLEDGEMENTS 9

1. POWER OF THE PENCIL 11
Notes 21

2. ILLITERACY: A PARADOXICAL INHERITANCE 23
A Betrayal of History 23
The Fireplace Of Culture 25
Oppression Through Illiteracy 31
Darkness To Light 35
Notes 36

3. A COMPLEX OF LANGUAGES 37
1974: Before and After 38
Language and the New Constitution 39
A Nation–wide Language 42
Language and Pedagogy 45
Dialects: A Continuing Issue 46
Notes 49

4.'LET EVERYBODY LEARN!':
THE BEGINNINGS OF THE CAMPAIGN 51
A Policy of Parsimony 51
The 1974 Revolution 53
The First Steps Towards Mass Literacy 55
Objectives 56
An All–inclusive Structure 57
A Compulsory Programme 59

The First 'Rounds' 60
Notes 62

5. THE YOUTH GALVANISED 63
Secondary School: Preparing For Democracy 63
Training for the Campaigners 65
The Impact of REYA 66
The Process of Identification 67
Building A New Youth 69
Notes 71

6. ORGANISING THE WORD 73
From Kitchen to Literacy Class 74
Reading Close to Life 75
The Dynamo of REWA 76
Letters in the Light 80
From the Plough to the Pen 83
'Let us have our school!' 84
Notes 85

7. A PEOPLE'S PEDAGOGY: THE CAMPAIGN IN SIDAMO 87
Briefing in Awassa 87
A Teacher Speaks of Literacy 89
The Work of one Kebele 90
'The Grass Itself Speaking' 92
Early Morning in Boditi 94
'Fill the Environment with Letters!' 95
'Let Everything be Used!' 99
On to Ade Aro 101
'If the Drought Comes Again' 102
Notes 104

8. LITERACY AND AFTER 105
Struggling Against Relapse 108
Strategies for Post–literacy 109
A Literate Environment 110
Notes 112

About the Author

Chris Searle is an English writer, teacher and poet who has worked in London, the Caribbean, Mozambique and Sheffield. He has written such works as *The Forsaken Lover: White Words and Black People*, which won the Martin Luther King Award in 1972, *Classrooms of Resistance* (1975), T*he World in a Classroom* (1977), a collection of short stories *The Black Man of Shadwell* (1976) and *We're Building the New School*! (1981) about a secondary school in Mozambique. His poems are included in *Mainland* (1974), *Red Earth* (1980) and *Common Ground* (1983). *Sunflower of Hope* (1982) is his collection of translated poems from the Mozambiquan Revolution.

He is also author of *Words Unchained: Language and Revolution in Grenada*, Zed Press and *Grenada Morning: a Memoir of the 'Revo'*, Karia Press, 1989.

He is the editor of *Young World Books* and has either translated or edited *Tales of Mozambique*, *Ngunga's Adventures*, *Callaloo*, *Our City*, *All our Words* and *One for Blair*.

Glossary

awraja	administrative district
birr	unit of Ethiopian currency
cloze	a 'filling in the gaps' written exercise
EPA	Revolutionary Organisation of Ethiopian Peas ants
Ge'ez	ancient language of the Ethiopian church
injera	Ethiopian food made from *teff*
kebele	urban dwellers' association
orthography	spelling system
pedagogy	method and process of teaching and learning
REWA	Ethiopian Revolutionary Women's Association
REYA	Ethiopian Revolutionary Youth Association
shengo	parliament
syllabary	'alphabet' of syllables
teff	staple cereal crop of Ethiopia
wereda	administrative sub–district

Mural on house in Ade Offa village

ACKNOWLEDGEMENTS

This short account could never have been written without the close cooperation and support of the colleagues of the National Literacy Campaign of Ethiopia. I have leant very heavily, in particular, on the scholarship of two outstanding educators: Mammo Kebbede Shenkut, the Executive Officer of the Campaign and Neway Wolde Sadik, its former Chief of Administration and Finance. I also thank other colleagues at the Adult Education Department of Ethiopia's Ministry of Education: Getahun Kebede, Giday Lemma, Tessema Mersha, Alemseged Bezabeh, Yeman Ayele, Folke Albinson, Ibrahim Sayed, Haile Shemer and Getachew Kelemu.

Shifferaw Encubahry, Gedamu Dessie, Teshome Mersha and Getachew Awoke all showed warmth and friendship to me during our time together in Sidamo, and I thank them for it. I would also like to thank Mengistu Edo of REYA, Yohannes Beraki and Damtew Gebru who gave me invaluable insights into the activities of the Ethiopian youth, Asegedech Bezuneh the REWA chairperson and Nigat Mengesha, Head of REWA'S Foreign Relations service. Abdela Sonessa, the Chairman of EPA, gave of his time most generously in order to brief me about the Ethiopian peasants' movement. I would also like to thank very sincerely the officals of the Ministry of Information and the Ministry of Education, and the Central Committee of the Workers' Party of Ethiopia. I also thank Tsegaye Gebre Medhin for his invaluable background to Ethiopia's history and culture.

I owe a particular debt to Tefera Endalew, Administrator of Sidamo Region, both for his hospitality and for the pen which he gave me — with which I have, as promised, written what follows. I would also like to thank other Sidamo colleagues: Gebre Michael Challa, Administrator of Wollaita Awraja and Dawit Likassa Bulcha, Administrator of Arero Awraja. Also Bezabeh Shibeshi, Dereje Bekkele, Dawit Shumbulo and all the students, teachers and cadres who showed me their friendship and huge professional skills. This book is simply one other small side–result of their hard work and genius, and I hope that it also salutes their achievements.

In England I have been much helped by Dr Teshome Teklu, Ms Kay Gallagher and His Excellency Teferra Haile Selassie, the Ethiopian Ambassador in London. I have also been supported by those two ageless stalwarts of Liberation, Kay Beauchamp and Tony Gilbert. My thanks are also extended to colleagues of the Sheffield Education Department, to W.S. Walton, Brian Wilcox and Councillor Joan Barton in particular, and to Sally Long for her exemplary typing. I would also like to thank my wife Pearl and my children Victor, Kevin, Daniel and Russell for their patience and forbearance during my nights of work on this short book

Finally, any errors the reader may discern are totally my responsibility; any sense of enthusiasm that may be communicated is the result of the inspiration of the people of Ethiopia and the children and teachers of Sheffield.

The people of Sheffield on the march for literacy in Ethiopia.

1.
POWER OF THE PENCIL

Perhaps no other human catastrophe since the Second World War has had such a profound effect on the minds and imaginations of Europeans, as the 1984-5 drought and famine in the northern regions of Ethiopia. It provoked the best and the worst in the European character and its attitudes towards Africa. People thousands of miles away from those suffering in the afflicted areas ran races, swam miles, played music, fasted, danced, sold their property, organised family–wide to school–wide, nation-wide to worldwide fund–raising events, and gave spontaneously and with huge waves of human solidarity to African people struggling against hunger and destitution. With the help of such international humanitarian assistance, millions of lives were saved in Ethiopia.

Yet accompanying this outpouring of trans–world friendship and compassion were often less worthy energies and more sinister intentions. Powerful forces in Europe and North America were seeking to create advantage from tragedy. As the government and entire population of Ethiopia, propelled by a revolutionary commitment towards their own huge majority who had lived for seemingly endless years with the backwardness of the old feudal regime – were mobilising themselves to fight the effects of the disaster, a chorus of hostility towards the Ethiopian people and their Revolution sang out in the European media. The *Times* and the *Sun* of London, using different words and styles but both speaking with the voice of the News International corporation and its proprietor Rupert Murdoch, waded in to insult the Ethiopian government and its leader, Mengistu Haile Mariam. In a nefarious feature article called 'Famine's fatal combination — red tape, gold braid', the *Times* accused the Ethiopian government of diverting aid resources to its favourite projects (10 November 1984). Over three years later when a further severe drought threatened, the *Sun* tried to deter its readers from sending humanitarian aid contributions to Ethiopia, asserting that emergency relief for the Ethiopian people was 'an exercise in futility' which only prolonged the period of power of a 'pitiless tyrant' (2 December 1987). Punning upon the name of a well–known international relief agency, the *Sun* declared in its editorial of that issue: 'War on Won't : (They won't do anything for themselves.)' Such contemptuous statements about this long–struggling people had been meat and drink to much of the British press since the very outbreak of the famine, with the very conservative British weekly, the *Spectator* (1 December 1984) perhaps plummeting to the lowest and most absurd depths of all in the title of its feature article on Ethiopia, even accusing Mengistu of causing the famine himself!

Yet the words of the *Sun* had become insistent and thematic in British media coverage of the famine: 'They won't do anything for themselves.' For many Europeans had become so besotted by the force of their own charity that they actually believed and parroted them. The idea they expressed took on the form of a vicious and anti–African racist myth: 'these people cannot help themselves. They are entirely dependent upon us, just as they always have been. They are still the white man's burden.' No publicity was given in Britain, for example, to the massive national effort of relief and rehabilitation organised within Ethiopia itself through the Ethiopian government and its structures, to remove the problems faced by its own people. As Mengistu himself, in a nationwide broadcast, called upon 'all Ethiopians who champion the cause of justice and common prosperity' to rally to support their stricken compatriots, a number of critical measures were taken. Contributions of money from wage earners commensurate with their salary were organised nationally, a shift system was established for service at the relief centres around the nation, a ban was introduced on the import of cars, luxury items and textiles, with constraints on the use of petrol in order to maximise its use for transport within the famine areas. As the Ethiopian people gave large proportions of what they owned and earned to help the victims of the famine, 15,000 cadres from the Workers Party of Ethiopia, and thousands more workers from the Ministries of Agriculture and Health as well as members of the mass organisations of youth, women, the peasantry and the trade unions were deployed in the relief centres and in the re–settlement villages — where they were joined by 25,000 students, teachers and university and college lecturers. The epic voluntary migration of half a million people within the 1984–5 period, organised through the government's Relief and Rehabilitation Committee, from the unliveable areas of the arid north to the re–settlement villages in the more fertile and life–sustaining regions of South–western Ethiopia, had been made possible by the enormous work of preparation achieved by the people of the host regions for their battered compatriots. This life–saving process was reviled in the British press and compared to Hitler's herding of European Jews into concentration camps![1]

During the ten–month period from October 1984, food relief was distributed to 7.5 million sufferers from drought and famine. 1,500 kilometers of feeder roads were constructed to open up the new re–settlement areas and 200,000 houses and social centres were built. 530 tractors were transported for use in the new settlements and 1.2 million hand tools and 19,000 plough oxen were distributed to the new settlers. There was an intense national mobilization to counter the effects of the famine and a highly resourceful, well–prepared and profoundly humane strategy of long–term re–settlement to offer a new life to its victims. Yet to the British press, here was a people 'who won't do anything for themselves.'[2]

For very little reporting and evidence of the monumental efforts of the Ethiopian people, their revolution and their government during their time of national disaster ever appeared in the large–circulation European newspapers. Perhaps it suited those who preferred to indulge in self–congratulatory charity to keep it that way. For while the media remained silent about what the Ethiopian people were doing to help themselves, thunderous publicity accompanied the large–scale charitable enterprises organised in Europe. Huge reputations were made out of Africa's tragedy as European saints and knighthoods were created — particularly if the trumpeted and televised acts were spiced up with a few insulting or hostile words about the Ethiopian Revolution or government, or suggestions that unless the aid distribution was scrupulously supervised it would be siphoned off within Ethiopia before it reached the victims of the famine.

As a teacher, one of my main interests during this period was the effect that the exposure of Ethiopia and its people was having on the minds of children at school. It soon became apparent that an entire generation of British — and European — children, vulnerable as they were to the relentless transmission through television of desperate images of starving, skeletal human beings stricken with disease and continually beset by millions of flies — were internalising Ethiopia and Africa itself as a nation and continent of chronic disaster, dependence and uselessness. Before I made a visit to Ethiopia in 1986 to attend a conference organised by the World Peace Council, my seven year old son pleaded with me not to go, as he was convinced that there was no food in the country and I would starve. A new version of racist name–calling was developing in British playgrounds, around the contemptuous use of the word 'Ethiopian' for black children. That proud, culture–laden and history–filled word was being transformed into a word of pathos and insult by children who only knew one repeated and negative image of Africa.

That same image was reinforced time after time, day after day, in their profiles of Ethiopia taken from what they saw on their parents' television screens, and in the aftermath of the charity furores and spectacles that they had lived through. In their minds existed a grotesque collective profile of an Africa that was degraded, passive, static in poverty, hunger, nakedness and disease. Here are some of the typical words that some twelve year old children from the city of Sheffield in England, wrote about Ethiopia in 1988:

> Ethiopia is a place that poor people are. Some are starving and some have got some food. Their bellies stick out and you can see their bones and many people die.
>
> Ethiopia is a very small place, very little food and drink, hardly any clothes to wear, not many crops and animals and people dying and getting thin.
>
> I know that Ethiopia is a very poor country and that the people are very poorly educated. In Ethiopia there is very little food so lots of people are dying everyday of starvation.
>
> Ethiopia has not got a lot of money. They are starving. It is a place in Africa and Bob Geldof raised money for them.
>
> Ethiopia is a very hot place. They are starving. They have pot bellies not because they're fat but because they have no food. We try to help them by sending food to them, and clothes and other materials. They're poor.

And so it went on and on. Child after child had the same things to say, each time a message of despair and dependence. When asked about their sources of this thin knowledge, again it was always the same: television news programmes and documentaries, children's presentations like *Blue Peter* and *Newsround* — or their parents' newspapers owned by the giant press multinationals, like the *Sun*, the *Star*, the *News of the World* or the *Daily Mirror*. There was absolutely nothing that was positive in what they knew of

Ethiopia and Africa, nothing that showed dignity, humanity, determination or struggle. Nothing that showed any recognition or a spark of knowledge of the canon of Ethiopian achievement and culture, any understanding of the continuity of this great nation's unconquered history or its contribution as one of the cradles of human civilization.

This context of an educational and informational onslaught against a nation and its entire people, prompted by a national disaster which is distorted to become the entire reality of that people's lives and being – for the greater comfort and security of a post–colonial power — puts a very serious responsibility onto the work of teachers. Teachers have not been responsible for this terrible caricature of Ethiopia and Africa in the minds of their students, yet they have the task of transforming it towards balance and truth.

In 1986, during a brief visit to Addis Ababa, I had the opportunity to discuss with colleagues at the Ministry of Education the progress of Ethiopia's National Literacy Campaign. I recorded a long interview with Neway Wolde Sadik, an adviser in Adult Education and acting head of the campaign. As he spoke, giving insights into the literacy work and the huge effort of people's mobilisation that was enabling it to be successfully delivered to millions of Ethiopians, he communicated a fire of enthusiasm. I asked how we could help in Sheffield, where I worked in the city's Education Department.

The answer was simple and concrete: pencils! The campaign was being hampered in its work by a shortage of pencils. At the present time, Ethiopia has no way of manufacturing its own pencils. They needed to be imported, sapping invaluable foreign exchange. So in Sheffield we were presented with the gift of an opportunity to show our support and solidarity with a unique educational process that was experiencing a high level of success – so much so that it had won the UNESCO International Readers Association Award after its first year of operation in 1980. And while doing this we could also give our children an understanding of how Ethiopians were transforming their own lives through their own creativity, dedication to each other and organisational power. We could begin to counter and repair the damage of the *Sun* and the miles of film footage which had portrayed the Ethiopian people as helpless and eternally dependent.

In this way the 'lowly pencil', as one of our teachers termed it during a school assembly when the children were being thanked for raising over £700 for the campaign that we launched, became our symbol. It was a plain and simple symbol, the means through which our own children too had come to writing, as solid, useful and yet as unspecial as anything in their lives. We raised a slogan: 'one million pencils for Ethiopia!' and our support programme for Ethiopia's epic literacy campaign was born. So while the Ethiopian people counted their newly–literate graduates, we counted the money for pencils that we were sending them. With the commitment to the project of thousands of school students, teachers and parents, fund–raising events were organised through schools all over Sheffield, together with curriculum initiatives which showed the literacy campaign in action, its complex problems and the inventive solutions that Ethiopians were bringing to an inheritance of backwardness. We learned that as recently as 1979, as few as 7% of the Ethiopian population (which was established as 42 million people after the 1984 census), were literate. Yet we also learned that after nine years of concentrated literacy education, with entire communities all over Ethiopia mobilised to teach and learn — and during that same period of devastating drought and famine too — the level of literacy had been raised to 75.3%.

Involvement in the Sheffield support campaign has often meant a deeply moving experience. Children from first and infant, junior, middle, comprehensive and special schools from many parts of the city devised many original fund–raising activities which revealed a similar level of of inventiveness and organisational skill to their counterparts, the young literacy campaigners of Ethiopia. In one small middle school the students raised several hundred pounds by a combination of skateboard and cycle racing, a sponsored long–distance run and a sponsored knit. In a secondary school other young Sheffielders organsied a sponsored clean–up of their school together with a fancy–dress carnival. In another school the students sold apples donated by a parent who was also the local greengrocer. Almost an entire school population raised over £200 in a week by foregoing their mid–morning snacks and offering their money to the campaign: two middle schools combined in a sponsored walk across the north of Sheffield on a frozen February Sunday. One particular Pakistani boy raised £20 personally, having been moved to remember the illiterate in his own country of origin. In another nursery–infant school, the predominantly Punjabi–speaking mothers organised a cake sale, and a number of schools donated the proceeds of their harvest festivals. One nine year old girl danced non–stop for three hours to her favourite record and raised a considerable sum, and the students of another middle school raised £70 through a sponsored 'spell'. A comprehensive school, reflecting the way in which Ethiopian school students were teaching literacy skills to their own mothers and fathers, organised computer classes for parents. They charged a small subscription fee for these lessons, which was paid to the 'Pencils for Ethiopia' fund.

Among the most heart–felt contributions was that made by a school for children with severe learning difficulties. Many of these students have handicaps so formidable that they may never learn how to read and write themselves. Yet they strove to help ensure that people thousands of miles away from them in Ethiopia would master their own national languages and achieve literacy.

In a school for children with reading and communication problems, the Ethiopian Literacy Campaign proved to be a vehicle which helped the students express their own difficulties with language itself. A session on the campaign moved one boy to write about his own fear of words which appeared to have no coherence:

Strange Words

Here I am, lost again.
Nothing's going right.
I can't read, and the six year–old
Has beaten me alright.
He's on the hundredth page.
Those strange symbols
Odd things
Take me by the throat.
I'm full of rage and hatred too.
Rip them out!

Another boy in the same group, remembering the struggle and frustration of illiterate people in Ethiopia and their use of the thumbprint instead of a written signature to express their identity, transposed his own situation in Sheffield to theirs in Africa:

The Confusion of Words

A word is a funny thing.
I was sitting, totally in space,
Seeing a word, one I had seen before,
Maybe a thousand times.
I didn't know

What these symbols could mean.
My friends were on the end books.
I was on the first books.
It was sort of awkward,
And humiliating.
It was like putting a thumbprint
instead of a name.

Such priceless solidarity has often come from Sheffield children whose families have very little money themselves, from working class homes where parents are unemployed and where conditions of life are anything but easy. Yet such has been the force of these children's generosity and unforced internationalism that their actions and insights have overpowered the crude and blighted vision of the Ethiopian people that has been consistently presented to them by the most powerful media merchants in the world. Many Sheffield children are now exchanging letters with children in Ethiopia, and schools are establishing links between two continents.

Here, some seven year old children from a school in Tinsley, one of the most shattered areas of Sheffield's East End, surrounded by the remnants of the city's once famous and flourishing steel industry — reach out to the literacy students of Ethiopia in a short collective poem:

We hope the pencils will help you to do clever work.
We hope you use the pencils well.
We hope you have got sharpeners for the pencils.
We hope the pencils are good for the work you do.
We hope you have got some paper to write on.
We hope if the pencils break we could send you some more.
We hope you use the pencils to do numbers.
We hope you use the pencils to write stories.
We hope you use the pencils to draw pictures.
We hope the pencils will make you happy.

This support programme has not been an act of charity for 'unknown and unfortunate souls' in Africa. It has much more the character of a campaign of solidarity with African brothers and sisters engaged in a nation–building and life–changing process, created by British students and teachers in a spirit of equal endeavour. So much so that sometimes the Sheffield children's identification with the struggling people of Ethiopia in the midst of their popular explosion of education, has been almost total in some of the poems that they have written. As a group of junior school children wrote,

Children of Philmore Park Junior School, Sheffield, with their contribution to the 'Million Pencils for Ethiopia' campaign.

making it difficult to discern whether they were writing about Ethiopians or themselves:

Please help us to learn,
End the misery in our world.
Now is the time we must learn.
Concentrate and work hard,
Illustrate and write –
Listen to our words,
Support us!

Pencils help us write,
Education is important.
Now is the time to learn.
Concentration, determination,
I want to be
Literate!
Support us!

Peace for the future,
Education for all!
Now we have determination
Could it be?
I want to learn!
Literate is the word –
Support us please !

And in a message composed to accompany the presentation of a batch of 30,000 pencils for the campaign, a school student from Sheffield's Yemeni community read out in her pride and solidarity, the thoughts and sentiments of thousands of the city's young people:

> We, at Earl Marshal Comprehensive School, Sheffield, are proud to have the opportunity of helping our brothers and sisters in Ethiopia, and in particular of hosting this occasion. We hope that these pencils will assist in furthering your education. Education is important to us because we believe that through it power can be acquired to realise hopes and aspirations.
>
> We hope these pencils will be a symbol of our thoughts, and we extend our love and friendship towards you, our brothers and sisters in Ethiopia.

Such is the particular human context from which this short book has emerged. It also has, of course, a much wider context, that of an intensely difficult period when the Ethiopian Revolution was seeking to consolidate itself and move forward in the face of many hostile and destabilising forces intent on bringing it down —

thus paralleling the experiences of other revolutionary processes of the same era in Angola, Mozambique, Nicaragua and Grenada. For with the international media blitz against it, the Ethiopian process had also to face and survive a decade of horrendous natural catastrophes in its northern and south–western regions, including severe droughts, flooding and a plague of locusts. Secessionist conflicts in northern regions of the country were being fanned by hostile powers in and outside of the Middle East and the Horn of Africa, and development aid sanctions from some of the world's richest nations like Britain and the USA were in full force. And this while the Thatcher government of Britain was refusing to apply trade sanctions to Apartheid South Africa because it claimed that black South Africans would be those who would suffer! The same argument, of course, was not applied to the stoppage of development support for Ethiopia. The country was also recovering from the effects of repulsing an attempted invasion from a neighbouring nation, Somalia, to its east. Ethiopia's literacy achievement thus took place within the midst of the totality of these pressures and their consequences.

I was invited to visit Ethiopia for a second time in October 1988 in order to gain a greater understanding of the literacy campaign in action. I am a lucky man to have had the opportunity to talk extensively with and learn from some of Africa's most seasoned and brilliant adult educators, who have devised and organised the operation of this literacy campaign in offices, schools and centres in cities, towns and villages all over Ethiopia. For their work, in bringing light to so many millions of their compatriots in so many of their national tongues, can truly be described as an educational epic. Yet this effort, if we remember the *Sun* editorial, has come from a people who 'won't help themselves.'

It is to these colleagues in Ethiopia, their striving and success, and to the equally radiant humanity of our children here in Sheffield, that this book is dedicated.

Notes

1. See *The Challenges of Drought: Ethiopia's Decade of Struggle in Relief and Rehabilitation*: The Relief and Rehabilitation Commission, Addis Ababa, 1985; and *The Ethiopian Famine* by Kurt Jansson, Michael Harris and Angela Penrose, Zed Books, London 1987.

Both these books give a detailed and objective account of the 1984–5 emergency relief operation within Ethiopia.

2. See *Ethiopia's Campaign Against Famine: Resettlement and Rehabilitation* by John Clarke, Harney and Jones, London 1986, for a full description and assessment of the Ethiopian resettlement strategy.

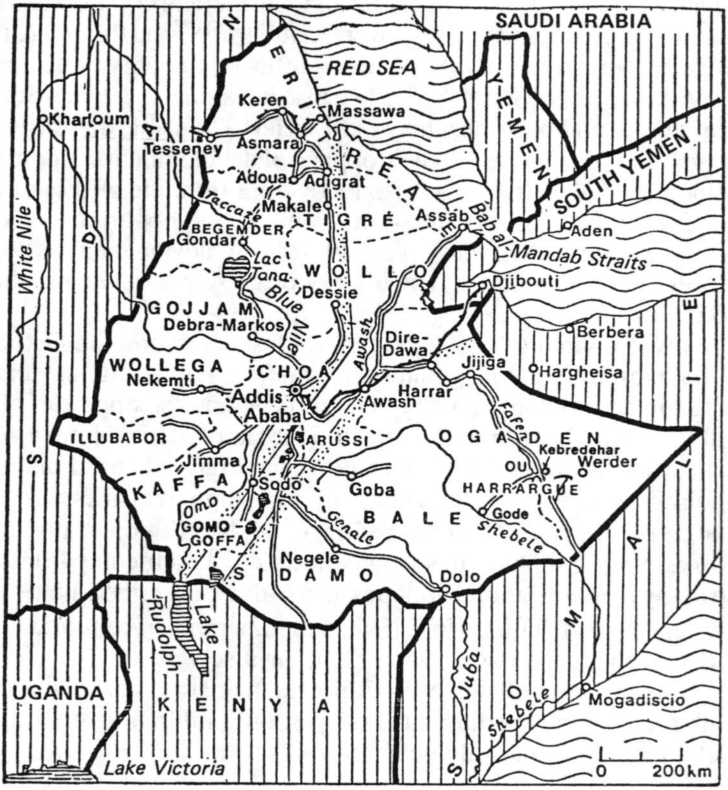

ETHIOPIA

Towns, provinces, railways and main roads
The Rift Valley, running through the centre of the country, is indicated.

2.
ILLITERACY: A PARADOXICAL INHERITANCE

Even though Ethiopia, following Egypt, has the second oldest written language in Africa which was commonly used across the vast land in large numbers of churches and monasteries, in 1974, in the twilight of its feudal rule, it had one of the highest illiteracy rates in the world. Only 7% of the population could read and write in a nation whose social history goes back to three and a half million years before the birth of Christ, from which time human remains have been found in long–buried settlements along the Awash River valley.

That 93% of Ethiopia's people should have faced such a monumental barrier to their human, economic and political development, was just one dimension of the feudal system under which they lived until the revolutionary events of 1974, which followed the imperial regime's failure to respond with any kind of commitment to the devastating effects of the 1973–4 famine. For at the watershed of its revolution, Ethiopia was one of the least developed countries in the world. The most basic health services were only available to15% of the population and only 2% of the entire people had any access to drinking water. Only 15.3% of Ethiopia's children had entry to any form of primary education, 6.8% to junior secondary and 3.4% to senior secondary schools. Primary agricultural production completely dominated the country's economy, with the manufacturing sector contributing only 5% to the gross domestic product. And yet only 14% of the potentially arable land was being cultivated, with the vast and realisable resources for irrigation and hydraulic power remaining unexploited. Of the estimated irrigable land of three million hectares, less than 3% had been developed.[1]

A Betrayal of History

Thus the considerable achievement of Ethiopia's ancient history and culture had been betrayed by its latter day feudal rulers. The huge cultural foundation laid down by early Ethiopian scholars, linguists, architects, engineers, artists and social organisers had been left to moulder in the decades before 1974. The civilisation that had erected the architectural marvels of the Axum obelisks in the seventh and eighth centuries, that had hewn churches out of solid rock in Lalibala in the tenth century, that had developed such a rich literary achievement through its own highly developed linguistic system – using Ge'ez, the parent language of Amharic – which flowered in the late middle ages, that had constructed the massively elegant castles in Gondar in the seventeenth century — this same civilisation had been allowed to languish to such an extent by its last emperor, that so few of its people could even read about its past glories in a history book.

Ethiopia was also the one African nation that had retained its political independence and territorial integrity, resisting attempts by the British, Turks, Egyptians and Italians during the most intense period of European expansionism and colonialism, to bring it under foreign rule. Between 1835 and 1935 the Ethiopian people had fought thirty four wars against external aggressors – which had often been led or orchestrated by the designs of British imperialism. In 1855 the Emperor Tewodros killed himself on the battlefield of Magdala rather than surrender to the British General Napier, and in 1887 the victory of the Ethiopian armies led by Ras Alula over the Italian invaders presaged the decisive repulse of 1896. In this year at Adwa, Emperor Menelik's forces secured the total defeat of yet another Italian army.

During the years of Italian fascist barbarism against the Ethiopian people after Mussolini's invasion of 1935 and the flight of Emperor Haile Selassie, the Ethiopian patriots never stopped organising and resisting. So much so that the occupying forces could never relax their grip or assume that they securely controlled any part of the country. This period of heroic resistance stayed fast in the consciousness of the people and was later to inspire a whole generation of Ethiopian revolutionaries, many of whom had inherited an intense patriotism and hatred of oppression from their parents and grandparents who had resolutely stood up against Mussolini. It was during this period of occupation too, that the few schools which had been established by the feudal regime (only 21 government schools throughout the country with a total of 4,200 students), were closed down by the Italian administration. The majority of the very small number of educated Ethiopians did not survive the harshness of this foreign rule, and existing minimal literacy was all but wiped out across the land.[2]

The Fireplace Of Culture

Yet despite the failure of its imperial regime to constructively build upon the glory of its past history and cultural tradition, Ethiopia has for long been an inspiration to the rest of Africa and the black and colonised peoples of the world precisely because of its unceasing determination to resist colonial rule and never surrender its unique cultural and linguistic patrimony and independence. The roots of this fierce pride and resistance have been expressed continuously by the nation's poets, visual artists and dramatists, who have kept Ethiopia's heroic tradition alive in their works. Such a figure is the national poet and playwright, Tsegaye Gebre Medhin, whose experience as Director of Ethiopia's national theatre and authorship of many classic plays and epic poetry in Amharic including the celebrated *Tewodros*, which has been translated into English and successfully performed on the London stage — has made him Ethiopia's best known literary artist. Tsegaye Gebre Medhin has also sought to bring significant European dramatic works to Ethiopia, and reduce the international cultural isolation faced by its people, while simultaneously affirming the strength and genius of Ethiopian culture and language. Thus he has translated into Amharic the works of Moliere, Brecht and Shakespeare (including *Tartuffe, Mother Courage, Lear, Hamlet, Othello* and *Macbeth*), as well as writing many works on African and Ethiopian culture and anthropology.

I interviewed him in Addis Ababa in June 1986 at the Ministry of Culture, where he works as an adviser.

How would you analyse the relationship between African and European culture?

One of the aspects of our cultural and political struggle in Africa has been to make Europe aware that many of the motifs and elements of music, dance and culture generally that are a part of European Society have arisen from this continent. This has been so ever since the beginning of humanity, for our continent, and Ethiopia specifically, was the cradle of humanity. The African was not waiting for the Greek or Latin culture to begin in order to mimic it. On the contrary, the earliest population of humanity started out from this continent, and made a contribution to human development which later societies picked up later in history in many of their cultural elements. So there was jazz, calypso, even the dancing and singing of the Rolling Stones, even the form of the costumes, their beads and hair–do — none of this is fundamentallly European. It is from our dances and music that they take. Thus Africa has always supplemented European culture, particularly during its time of bankruptcy.

It is this reality that has so often been continually ignored by Europe: it is not Africa playing up to Europe or taking imitation from its culture. Europe has grown from humanity in Africa — this is scientific reality, this is archaeology. This is where man first discovered language. Humanity was here in Africa before Europe or Asia were ever populated. And it has always been the right of all human beings of the world to seek their origins, to come back to earth and make peace with themselves in the sense of knowing their cradle, knowing where their personalities began to take form and where their culture as human beings started. It is the denial of this process that has been man's greatest ethnocentric problem and makes our struggle very difficult. The chronological and cultural reality is not faced by Europe, the chronological reality of the beginning of humanity and the making of the first settlements of humanity , where people sat together after the hunting and fishing and then discovered the first miming and then the first words, the first language and later the first city — Naqada, in the south of Egypt.

As man spread out through the Red Sea and the Mediterranean he formed the basis of the European and Asiatic man. European man did not come out of a vacuum, he came from a continuity with his cradle here in East Africa. Therefore this area of the world and its history, where the first human being lived, first danced and uttered language, first lived in cities, first made an alphabet and created culture is a common heritage of humanity, is universal heritage. And it is this very universality that is denied by Europe, and its ethnocentricity which seeks not only to disregard, but also to destroy that history. Our oneness, our human oneness has been distorted and a denial has taken place. The European tried to conceive of himself dropped from somewhere else, and denied his own link with Africa, his own continuity.

This fundamental denial is at the root of the problem which we are facing today. European man does not have the courage to face his own face! The idea of being born from an African, of coming from that root, "How could that happen?" asks the European. And he rejects it with ethnocentric dogma, with a pettiness, with an imposition of a false 'super–culture'. How could the imperial European man admit to himself that his roots were in Africa? Yet if your child and our child were taught about their true culture and the cradle from where they all started, which is their right, how we could begin to resolve this problem between the white man, the brown man, the black man, the yellow man! For the root of us all is one and the same and this knowledge and understanding is the right of all people of the world.

When you walk in our country, in the area of the southern lakes, in the Awash Valley where the oldest bones of man have been found dating back three or four million years, you are actually walking on the museum of antiquity, on the bones of the ancestors of all of us. This recognition is the first basis upon which we need to build in order to resolve this European ethnocentricity, this idea of the superiority of European culture which distorts history and separates us.

Take for example the case of our Ethiopian brothers and sisters the Falashas, whom, during the terrible time of hunger in the north of our country were claimed and taken over by the Israeli government claiming that they were different from me and other Ethiopians! This ridiculous ethnocentricity which asserts that an Ethiopian of the same blood, of the same origin is separate from me! Yet there is no historical evidence for this so–called difference. We are one, all of us.

So this kind of ethnocentric denial of African roots in Europe, of saying 'We have nothing to with you', has become a tradition that is cultural, spiritual and also a form of domination. By denying his own links and oneness with the African and the rest of humanity, Europe finds it easier to suppress and exploit that 'other' humanity. This is the source of the opposition to UNESCO now. The Director General M'bow is accused for telling Europe and the West 'you have not told us the truth about ourselves. We are re–discovering our own history. You have taken our iron ore, our copper and our diamonds. We have made the capitalists of Europe and America. Where has the material come to build your industry and aeroplanes? Where have you dug it from?' So these questions of the economic order, the cultural order, the information order started from the very beginning when the West began to deny itself against its own roots in Africa and refused to admit that it was an integral part of the cosmos. The European child is denied the self–awareness of knowing and understanding that he or she is part and parcel of the world and of Africa. The child is denied the link of knowing that he and I have the same origins, the same ancestors, a common heritage of culture. He is not

Tsegaye Gebre Medhin

taught this! That is the cultural and psychological oppression rested upon the mass of the western world, particularly the children.

How did the imperial powers attempt to attack the culture of the Ethiopian people, and what was the extent of the cultural resistance that was generated?

Sociologists and anthropologists have always told us that when two forceful cultures collide, two things happen. Firstly, people who live by their own culture and are identified by that culture, when the attack takes place will absorb and take in elements of that attacking culture. This Ethiopia has always done, but in doing it has always moulded the elements of this new aggressive culture with its own shape. It has assimilated it, and because this Ethiopian culture has been so forceful, those who come to conquer have as a result become Ethiopians themselves. When Christianity came to Ethiopia and we adopted it into our system, we made an Ethiopian form of Christianity which is completely different from any other form of the religion. For example, for the epiphany we carry the tabernacles on our head and we go to the river and sprinkle the holy water. Now sprinkling the holy water is a very ancient Hamitic tradition too. No other Christian tradition carries the tabernacle to the lake or the river, or has the burning of the cross. So we have taken Christianity, but through the strength of our own culture it has become Ethiopian. Whereas in other situations where the civilisation and culture are weak, the society upon whom a new European culture has been imposed has been too feeble to resist it and recreates towards the image of Europe. Thus the colonized man in this situation becomes internally very French, very British or very Arab. Only the skin remains, internally he's a different man, she's a different woman and he's taken over completely, becoming a foreigner, an artificial human being cut off from the root of history and tradition and putting himself politically on top of the people . This artifical creature , neither European or African, imposing his superficiality on the people, trusted by the people because of his African name and origins, is hardly anything of the people, is the personality created in the image of the imperalist and capitalist.

For three thousand years whoever came to conquer Egypt became Egyptian. This is even more true in relation to Ethiopians. This is why we have Arab Ethiopians, Greek Ethiopians, Armenian Ethiopians who could recite Ethiopian poetry more than I can. This is the face of Ethiopian culture that returns right back to that cradle of humanity. So that even in accepting Marxism into our system, we give it a tremendous element of the Ethiopian backbone, we make it even stronger. It is the people who embrace it! Not simply me, not simply the intellectuals but the mass of the people. That is why it survives and grows, because it has been adopted into that indestructible, concrete foundation of Ethiopian culture and tradition.

Mussolini and Italian imperialism before it, for example, being blinded by their ethnocentrism, said 'Go and conquer, civilize these barbarians in Ethiopia'. But they came up against the rock of our culture and failed, they were crushed by it. Yet at the same time the Ethiopians saw positive aspects in this imperialist culture from which we learned and which sometimes we adopted – the ability to build roads, for example – this was learned from the Italians.

How did the culture of the ordinary masses of the Ethiopian people resist the rule of the feudal powers in Ethiopia before the revolution?

The feudal rulers, the imperial force, claimed their roots from outside Ethiopia, outside of the African tradition and history, outside of the black origins of the masses. They said they came from the Solomonic root. They claimed a circle of their own that was separate from the tradition of the masses, a circle that the masses could not reach. By separating themselves in this way they managed their own continuity, a culture of oppression which declared: 'I am the elect of God, the Lion of Judah' – not of Ethiopia! While they made their separation complete, they affected the people's psychology in a negative way. The people knew they were of the same blood, knew their fathers and mothers, knew where they were born. So this imposed artificial culture of feudalism was one which was always questioned by our people because they knew exactly from where these feudal elements came.

So it is this exposure in the people's minds, this constant non–acceptance and questioning, that caused them never to accept this Solomonic culture of their rulers. They resisted because they know the lion is an African lion! It is scientifically African, it has never come from Asia or anywhere else but Africa. There is no lion in Judah, no lion in Britain either — except in the zoos. So the people knew that the lion is their animal, their symbol, a part of their culture, their identity and personality. They knew it to be a unique animal which has its origins in their part of Africa, even though you will find it used all over Europe in the heraldry and symbolism of European ruling classes — on the English coat–of–arms for example. Again it is Africa supplementing the bankruptcy of European culture.

But the people know in every aspect where their tradition and culture have been denied and stolen, their suspicion and insight which grew from day to day itself became a force. They realised through the strength and foundation of their own culture the artificiality of the culture which oppressed it and the economic force and exploitation behind it. This is why Ethiopian culture has stood out defiantly, because it is the root upon which Africa and the earliest man became himself. The cultural strength of the people has been incubated and protected in the cradle of the people's awareness. The people are not just singing, dancing and writing it, they are living it, in the form of their revolution. Life has been taken into their own hands and their new culture is its fireplace.

But we are still faced with a fierce and formidable enemy. In the period of colonialism the Ethiopian people resisted and defeated imperialism and retained their independence. Alone in Africa, Ethiopia was never colonised, it stood alone.

This example, the victories of Menelik against Italian imperialism, gave a certain spiritual force to the rest of Africa to do the same. This has been internalised by the oppressed peoples of the Third World. Now, when imperialism changed its face and created neo–colonialism as an alternative form, and Africa and the other oppressed continents face a new form of re–occupation by European and north America imperialism — then all of Africa is the front line. The war for our economic independence has already started, the war against this economic and cultural re–occupation that also penetrates by its imperialist information order. We're not talking about the multinational corporations, hunger or desertification, we're talking about South Africa and its apartheid regime, ally of imperialism, invading sovereign states, attacking them and expanding itself. So our national anthems and national flags are not the real issue. The imperialist is still with us, pushing us from South Africa, seeking to re–occupy us. We need a new African awareness of this, just as the period of Menelik was a huge source of the re–strengthening of the people, and that awareness is there, strong and resilient, indestructible as ever, in the foundation of our culture, as it has been there since the cradle of our beginning.[3]

Oppression Through Illiteracy

Thus the people of Ethiopia were left to struggle with their feudal rulers within this grim historical paradox: such a fertile cultural history, yet such a low level of literacy and educational opportunity. For Ethiopia was known before the revolution of 1974 as The

Land of the Scribe and the Thumb–print. The regular humiliation of having to ask another person to write your letters for you and invade your privacy and your most intimate messages and thoughts, or the public shame of not being able to sign your own name on basic legal documents or when drawing your wages, rested heavily on the mass of the people — particularly the peasantry that made up nearly 90% of Ethiopia's population. When they were arraigned in the courts of their landlords, ordinary Ethiopians could not even read or understand the charges levelled against them, neither could they easily defend themselves from cheating merchants who could fox them by their false calculations and trickery. It is not surprising that for Ethiopians, the almost universal image for illiteracy is darkness and that for literacy is the doorway of light. During the third year of the literacy campaign, in 1982, a poetry competition was organised. The winning entry, by Yohannes Shumye of Wollo region, eloquently expressed the reality of oppression through illiteracy and the entry into the light.

I started to Learn by Saying 'A'

When I remember the past power of the lords
And us having to wash their feet, light their candles,
serve them after their feasts–
Or early in the morning, before the birds sing
and the dawn breaks,
Opening their cattle pens, leading out the calves,
Saddling the mules for the lords and their ladies,
Carrying their holy books for them, following them
in procession to church,
Saying a prayer – not for myself, but for them,
Thanking God, as if this were a good life!

As the voice droned on from the holy script,
Yes, from the holy script
Chanted by the priest
The words of the prayers
Making circles round the compound of the church –
I was thinking that this, my God,
Only listens to those who can read and write,
The lords, the governors, the judges
and those at their level.

Feeling a huge pain and sickness
My blood spilling out,

'Under the National Literacy Campaign, the traditional use of the thumb–print will disappear!'

A Blindfold Removed: Ethiopia's Struggle For Literacy

Not even able to eat one single *injera,**
Living under hunger, misery and illiteracy –
I could not even tell God of all this suffering.

Anyway
Let's carry on thanking God for this!
Let the educated ones carry on with their holy words!
Let the emperor stay on his throne –
That's what I used to say in that time of darkness.

That long age – thinking of it today,
Remembering it through our struggle,
Now our people learning their alphabet –
The old, the young, the women, the soldiers –
Now all equals in their motherland,
Building their economy, cultivating their earth,
Learning their letters
Teaching and learning –
I started to learn by saying 'A',
Linking word to word
I started to read,
I started to read of the viciousness of my past,
I discovered history by being able to read it!
I found out why I had been downtrodden —

Illiteracy had oppressed me,
Knowing neither numbers nor letters
I was paying a quarter of my income in tax!
Illiteracy had oppressed me,
My labour and property were stolen from me.

Now, through the Revolution I have been re–born,
It has brought me light
It has brought me a harvest of literacy,
It is finishing with illiteracy
And the fruit of struggle is ripening.

All of us are coming to know our alphabet
The people are learning to read!

The educated teach the uneducated
And the struggle still goes on
until we reach socialism!

---

* *Injera:* Staple food of much of Ethiopia, made from an indigenous cereal crop called *teff*.

The cultural campaign is moving ever forward
The oppressors have been defeated
Because now we are educated![4]

Yohannes Shumye's poem expresses very strongly the sense of despair and impasse in the lives of millions of Ethiopians before 1974, who lived behind the bars of the imperial system and whose lives existed to cultivate for the landlords and the feudal state, and to fight in the contesting armies of the baronial lords. The Orthodox Chruch of Ethiopia saw its first interest with the state against any aspirations of the mass of the people, and kept a close circle of literates in the 'Houses of Learning' administered by the local priests in the church compounds. Very few Ethiopians benefited from the learning in the ecclesiastical language of Ge'ez, that the church kept to itself in an aura of religious mystery and exclusivity. It was only the scribes who retained any working knowledge of written language in the villages, as they had regular and professional recourse to it. For the few young Ethiopians who attended the priest schools and learned the fundamentals of literacy, the reality of their families' working lives made the plough and the hoe the instruments of their daily survival. Whatever literacy skills they had learned in the churchyards soon relapsed and became little more than childhood memories.

Darkness To Light

In the village of Ade Aro in the province of Wollaita–Sodo in October 1988, I met a thirty five year old peasant farmer called Aberra Pilto. Having recently become literate in his mother tongue, Wolayitigna, he had soon made the transition to Amharic and was reading an article about the new constitution in the newspaper of the Workers Party of Ethiopia, *Serto Ader* ('The Worker') in a post–literacy class. He told me, through an interpreter, how happy he felt as he could now read the newspaper from cover to cover and could also follow and understand the political and social content of the daily radio programmes. As he put it, 'I now know my country in a way I could never knew it before.' He also told me how he was beginning to take measures to preserve the soil on his plot of land, in order to counteract the damage done by years of erosion. He showed me the book he had been reading which instructed him in methods to effect this. When I asked him how he had felt before the literacy campaign when he was among the 93% of the population unable to read and write, he answered, very confidently, in his own Wolayitigna:

In those days I had to find someone to write letters for me and persuade them not to tell other people what I was saying in them. Sometimes these professional letter–writers were busy–bodies and told everyone in the village about your private affairs that you might put into your personal letters to your family or friends. I often felt shy and inferior, just going from place to place looking for someone I trusted to write a letter for me. I had to bring the paper and pencil to them too. And it would cost anything from fifty cents to a whole birr for a scribe to write just one letter.

Now I don't have to go through any of that shame. I sit at home and write my own letters now, and I don't have go tell anyone what I write if I don't want to. That is what the revolution and the literacy campaign has brought to people like me.

For millions of Ethiopians like Aberra Pilto the paradox of their illiteracy is being resolved. They can now claim with their own use of their own languages – and with a new capacity for learning and knowing – the massive heritage and dignity of their country's past, and of being an Ethiopian. And while doing this, they are involved in transforming its present and unlocking the rich potential of its future, for themselves and their children.

Notes

1. See *Ethiopia: Brief Review of some Achievements, Problems and Prospects in the process of the National Democratic Republic*, Legesse Lemma. (A paper presented at the International Round Table discussion on the 'Socio–economic Development of Black Africa and Problems of Democracy', sponsored by the Part of Independence and Labour (PIL — Senegal) in co–operation with the World Marxist Review, January 1986.
2. See Sbacchi, Albert, *Ethiopia Under Mussolini*, Zed Press, London 1985.
3. Interview with Tsegaye Gebre Medhin by Chris Searle, *African Times*, 25 December 1987, London.
4. I am indebted to Dawit Likassa Bulcha and Gedamu Dessie for the translation of this poem from Amharic.

3.
A COMPLEX OF LANGUAGES

What characterises the National Literacy Campaign of Ethiopia as a unique mass initiative is its multi–lingual structure and pedagogy. Fifteen of Ethiopia's eighty–plus languages are being used as teaching and learning languages in the campaign. In the first round of the programme five major languages were used: Amharic, Oromigna, Tigrigna, Wolayitigna and Somaligna. During Round Four, as the campaign moved into other language areas of the country, Hadiyigna, Gedeogna, Tigre, Kambatta and Kunama were also employed. By Round Seven, five more mother tongues were being adopted as Sidamigna, Silti, Afar, Kefa–Mocha and Saho were added to the campaign's languages of instruction.[1]

The only comparable approach in the history of literacy campaigns involving so many languages was the colossal enterprise of the campaign of the Soviet Union (1919–39), a country which in itself embraced 122 languages, and whose literacy programme offered the choice of language of instruction either as Russian or the learner's native language. At the outset of the beginning of the pioneer Soviet campaign, some 30% of the population were literate — a percentage which, despite its very low level, compares very favourably with Ethiopia's 7% in 1979.

To add to the complexity and difficulty of Ethiopia's languages situation, the country's languages themselves arise from at least four different sources. There are Semitic languages such as Amharic, Tigrigna, Tigre and Silti; Nilotic languages like Kunama; those of Kushitic origin such as Oromigna, Somaligna, Hadigna, Sidama, Gedeogna, Afar, Kembatta and Saho, and Omotic languages (with their origins in the lands around the Omo River in south–western Ethiopia) like Kefa–Mocha and Wolayitigna. These tongues, and many others, plus a network of dialects, make up the extraordinarily rich but complex fabric of languages spoken by the many nationalities of the Ethiopian people.

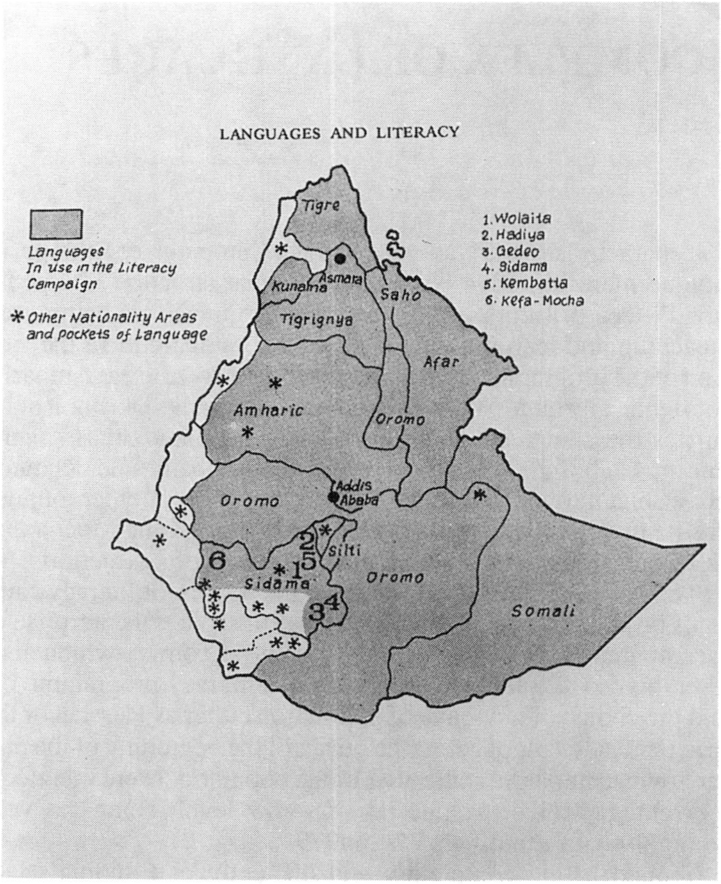

1974: Before and After

Before the Ethiopian Revolution in 1974, there was little opportunity for speakers of languages other than Amharic to explore and express the fullness of their tongues. Amharic was seen very much as the language of power, status and privilege. It had its origin as a language of the court, an aristocratic language spoken in the environs of palaces and offices of government by the imperial coterie and the high–ranking officers who were predominantly of Amharic nationality. As the language of the court, it grew gradually into becoming the language of the entire nation — as to gain favour, influence and custom with the highest in the land, it was necessary to speak Amharic. Thus it was adopted as the main language of instruction in the few primary schools that existed. Missionaries working within Ethiopia were required to learn and teach in Amharic, and were only allowed to use other languages of nationality in the early stages of their missionary work. Thus Amharic had a posiiton of primacy amongst the languages of Ethiopia.

Only Amharic and Tigrigna had their own scripts, newspapers and any tradition of written literature – although missionaries had attempted to transcribe the Bible into Oromigna.

The events of 1974 brought the promise of a complete rupture with the absolutism of the Amharic tongue. As a part of the Revolution's commitment that no one nation will dominate another, equal recognition was given to the history, culture, language and religion of every nationality. This was stated quite unequivocally in the programme of the National Democratic Revolution of Ethiopia issued in April 1976, which declared that each nationality has the right to determine the contents of its political, economic and social life, use its own langage and elect its own leaders and administrators to head its internal organs.

This pledge was already accompanied by solid actions. By 1975 the National Work Campaign for Development through Co–operation was using Oromigna, Tigrigna, Wolayitigna and Somaligna, in addition to Amharic for its literacy instruction, and was preparing to employ Hadigna, Sidamigna and Afar. By July 1978 the Ministry of Education had decided that in order for any literacy effort to effectively reach the mass of the Ethiopian people, the fifteen nationality languages eventually used in the National Literacy Campaign must be employed.

By this date, some serious research had been done on the linguistic complexity of Ethiopia, and its results had been published in a book called *Language in Ethiopia* by M. S. Bender. One of Bender's conclusions was that the selected fifteen languages were spoken by nearly 95% of the population, and that most of the other 5% were bilingual in, or could manage to understand at least one of them, as well as their own minority language.

Language and the New Constitution

Thus by September 1987, when the Constitution of the People's Democratic Republic of Ethiopia was ratified by the first assembly of the National Shengo (or parliament), the Constitution's declaration on languages was well on the way to being fulfilled through the monumental mobilisation of nationality languages that had been achieved through the literacy campaign:

> The People's Democratic Republic of Ethiopia shall ensure the equality, development and respectability of the languages of nationalities (*Article 2, sub–article 5*)

One of Ethiopia's pioneer adult educators, Neway Wolde Sadik, spoke these words about the Literacy Campaign's effect on those who have taken part, learning how to read and write in the language closest to their hearts and lives:

> As a result of the programme, Ethiopians have been able to feel that their nationalities are respected, linguistically and culturally, particularly when the government took the unprecedented step of creating the literacy programme in fifteen national languages. It has meant a new pride and confidence for the speakers of those languages. They now see and read their languages in a scripted form. They see alphabets being designed for what was previously only an oral language, they write in that language and see that it is equal to all other languages in the country, equal to Amharic too that used to be the language of domination.
>
> So the literacy programme has actually helped to develop languages and create alphabets and spelling systems in our country. All these languages are now in a written form as a result of our literacy programme and the government's policy of giving equal respect and support for all the languages of our nationalities. That too has been an achievement of the programme, to stress and manifest that all Ethiopians, no matter from what part of our country they come, are equal in language, in culture, in status and national identitiy. This has become one of our slogans: 'Equal in culture, equal in language', to destroy any idea in the past that one nationality, language or culture is superior to another. And this was a problem for us for over four hundred years while Amharic was used as the language of government and associated so strongly with organised religion.
>
> Take for example the mass discussion and consultations around our new national constitution. This can now go on in many languages, not only Amharic. Now so many more millions of our people can read the draft constitution in their own languages and play an active part in its development. For now they are literate! Fifteen languages are now being used to explain the constitution and obtain the comments of the people. Now many of the people who have been through our literacy programmes are helping to make the translations into these

languages. For them education has meant bringing more light into their minds, and they are adding to the voltage all the time.

In order to support this new policy and practice of setting free the languages of nationality from the neglect of the past, the National Academy of the Amharic Language (founded during the last years of the Empire, in 1972) was transformed into the Academy of Ethiopian Languages. One of its first responsibilities was to work co–operatively with the National Literacy Campaign in developing spelling systems founded upon the Ethiopian syllabary — as a priority in the languages of instruction of the campaign.

Mamo Kebbede Shenkut, the energetic and erudite Executive Officer of the campaign, made clear that the reasons behind the adoption of the fifteen nationality languages in the campaign are both pedagogical and constitutional.

> Our intention in using the nationality languages is first and foremost to effectively introduce to our students the skills of writing, reading and numeracy. This is much more easily achieved in their own first language, rather than Amharic if that is not their language. If they learn first in Amharic as a second language, they would have to jump over their own first language into one they do not know very well or may not know at all.
>
> But alongside this educational objective is our respect for our people's nationality languages. They need to develop these languages in order to maintain their traditional values and culture. And in the proposed Shengos at various levels, the people's own nationality languages will be used. At the National Shengo, many of these languages were used, and then translated back into Amharic for those people present who could not understand them.
>
> So one doesn't have to learn Amharic to be a member of the National Shengo, otherwise that would disenfranchise large numbers of our people.[4]

Yet Amharic as a language still has a vital unifying and compacting role to play in revolutionary Ethiopia. In the constitution, Amharic is known as the 'working language' of Ethiopia. It is not a 'national' language, although it is, of course, a nationality language to the millions of Ethiopians to whom it is their mother tongue. The question of what language should form the means of communication across the entire country and allow those for example in the Eritrean region of the north to communicate with those in Sidamo in the south, or the people of the western regions like Welega or Illubabor to speak to those living in Hararge on the borders of Somalia, was a vital question to be resolved. For although the consolidation of cultural identity, of tradition and history are vital issues affecting the choice of languages a nation makes for its people, that choice must necessarily consider the economic and political development of the entire nation and its people.

A Nation–wide Language

Some nations have been fortunate, in terms of access to mass literacy, to have a single language across their entire population which is a language of heritage and understanding. Thus their literacy campaigns have been waged in that single language that is also the mother tongue of all,or the vast majority of people. Countries such as Cuba, Brazil, Grenada and Burma, or Somalia and Tanzania on the African continent have all benefited greatly from this situation and avoided the organisational and cultural complexities of needing to serve literacy in a complex variety of languages. For these countries too, the adoption of a language across the whole population has been a natural process, managed without internal rancour — even though in the cases of Tanzania and Somalia, there were internal and external pressures to set aside their African tongue for the languages of the colonising powers. In Tanzania there was also the issue of whether to consolidate Kiswahili as the national tongue or to put greater support and emphasis upon the 150–plus tribal languages also spoken across the country. In the event of political independence in 1961, the bold decision for Kiswahili was made and widely supported.

But such decisions are never easy ones. Upon them the economic future as well as the cultural direction of nations are grounded. The choice of Portuguese, the language of the coloniser, for example, in the ex–colonies of Portugal like Mozambique and Angola, has maintained a sense of administrative and linguistic continuity for the state machinery in the new nations and consolidated Portuguese as the language of unity across cultural and tribal divisions (which was so vital and decisive during Mozambique's war of national liberation before independence in 1975). Yet for millions of people struggling for literacy in a language which may be their second and third tongue, without having had the opportunity to be literate in their mother tongue, difficult problems of learning have been created — and for their teachers, complex pedagogical issues.

In his book *Campaigning for Literacy*, a critical analysis of some literacy campaigns worldwide, which was submitted as a report to UNESCO in 1981, H.S. Bhola summarises some of these complexities.

> In the modern world of the nation–state based on science and technology and bureaucracy, one must know the language of politics for sharing power and the language of the economy for participation in the economic system. Literacy in a language other than the national language may doom one to a limited and parochial and marginal existence[5]

Thus a nation which is concerned with democratic progress, and which is engaged in a national democratic revolution, striving to bring its entire population into the process of participation in social and economic development — and seeing priorities in terms of building mass democratic organisations of women, youth, peasants and workers, to ensure this happens — must have recourse to a nationwide means of communication, as well as a policy which gives respect and confidence to its multiplicity of mother tongues. To satisfy both popular and developmental demands is not a simple process and often takes some hard, considered yet practical decisions for educators as well as policy creators. For whatever those decisions, and for the subsequent literacy efforts to work successfully, the pedagogy has to match both the political and linguistic realities. As Bhola wisely comments: "Clear strategies must be laid down about teaching literacy in the mother tongue and about later shift to the national language", (or in Ethiopia's case to Amharic, the working language).

In Ethiopia, which is the only African country south of the Sahara with its own writing system, co–operation between the Academy of Ethiopian Languages and the National Literacy Campaign organisers, created a common phonetic script for all Ethiopian languages, based upon Amharic. This fundamental step allowed what had been oral languages to take on a written expression and form the basis of mother–tongue literacy. While this work was progressing, the existing alphabet was revised, in order to bring together and cluster the symbols which had similar shapes, simplifying the process of learning the script for the literacy student.

As the Ethiopian script was syllabic in its notation rather than alphabetical, it offered a greater degree of textual economy through a smaller number of syllable types. This made it easier to learn, for both children and adult students.

Thus the written forms of the complex of languages across Ethiopia become uniformized in the manner of their expression on the page. So the movement from one language to another, and the transition from literacy in the mother tongue to post–literacy in Amharic as the common working language as well as the other languages of the campaign, was both facilitated and could be managed in the same syllabic script. This crucial crossing–point of languages was also helped by the daily reality of Amharic now being widely learned as a second language in many non–Amharic speaking parts of Ethiopia. Amharic was being constantly heard, used unevenly and partly understood, and adopted by Ethiopians throughout the entire country, as it was the language of commerce and officialdom, the language most used on the radio, and the language of instruction employed in primary school from grades one to six.

The language complexity in Ethiopia has been complicated to a further degree by the use of English as the language of instruction in schools from the seventh grade onwards. This has meant that many thousands of school children have had to move from their mother tongue to Amharic and then again to English within the first five years of their school life, even though a study of English only begins in grade three. Although Amharic had been introduced as the medium of instruction in some primary schools ten years before the Revolution, English had also been a medium of instruction. This put enormous strain upon any child who had not learned the language at a pre–school age. It necessarily excluded all but a tiny minority of Ethiopians from achievement in their early years of schooling.

Despite having to inherit the burden of such language problems and their resultant deformities within the national education system, the long–term objective of the Ministry of Education is to establish Amharic as the medium of instruction right through the school system, for adults too after the transition stage from the mother tongue to Amharic during the early phases of post–literacy education. Such a situation will clearly create much greater coherence in the system, as well as offer a common vehicle for democratic, political and economic progress across the entire country.

It appears the Ethiopians themselves fully recognise the need for such linguistic unity, as well as recognising the cultural strength that linguistic diversity gives to a nation with such a proud and rich history. When I asked Mammo Kebbede Shenkut whether there had been any concerted opposition or resistance to the planned development of Amharic as the main language in the post–literacy stages of education and beyond, his answer was quite emphatic: 'The situation is to the contrary of what you are asking. In many areas where the nationality language is not Amharic, the students have asked to study their literacy classes in Amharic because it is the medium of instruction for elementary schools. So if they want to continue their education in the formal system, then they have to be able to use Amharic. Many students want to start right away in Amharic, without becoming literate in their own mother tongue first'.

Language and Pedagogy

The pedagogy of the Literacy Campaign is itself to resist such leap–frogging of the nationality language, which could well hamper the learning of Amharic. The students at all times are encouraged to know the causes and effects of the conditions around them to 'read the word and read the world', as Paulo Freire pithily expressed it, in their own mother tongue, to consolidate their powers of conceptualisation and understanding of language itself, before eventually moving on to the post–literacy stage. Such a pedagogy also gives respect and understanding to the most intimate parts of a people's lives, the words of parents, grandparents and closest friends, the oral tradition of wisdom, song, proverb and folklore, the deepest and most heartfelt words of love and religious faith – all of which are messages spoken through the mother tongue.

These truths were well understood by the brilliant and extraordinary team of scholars and educators who organised the Ethiopian Literacy Campaign, all of whom had served an apprenticeship as teachers in classrooms in the regions of their vast country, and knew on their brains and pulses the concrete conditions that the campaign set out to change. These were teachers in the true sense of the word, professionals who had taught at the most elementary and local level, having to create their own resources and methods where little existed before through their inventiveness and determination. Thus their pedagogy did not simply come out of a book, to be transferred to their own classroom. It was forged in the context of teaching in the living and learning conditions of their own people. Such vital experience was then supplemented by more learning, scholarship and study, but always founded upon the issues provoked by their own country's educational reality. This is why their literacy campaign has been so monumentally successful: they know their people and their languages, having been a part of their processes of learning at the most fundamental level. Mammo

Kebbede Shenkut recalled his own teacher education in Majetie in North Shewa and Debre Birhan Teacher Training School: 'We were trained for two years on how to carry out literacy classes. We used to carry our small–size blackboards on our shoulders and go to the field in different directions to teach cattle–minders. We were given training not only in methodology but also in various useful skills like tanning, metal work, pottery, carpentry, weaving, gardening and dairy farming. However as soon as we graduated we remained simple primary school teachers.'

The work of Mammo Kebbede Shenkut himself arises from this deep experience of educating. As he says, 'the best pedagogic principles accepted and practised by various literacy experts involves the use of mother tongue for literacy purposes. Teaching literacy in an alien language means that in addition to the difficulties involved in learning the mechanics of reading and writing, the learner is further faced with the difficulties inherent in the acquisition of the vocabulary and the structure of words and sentences in that language .... literacy participants can understand their surroundings and accept new concepts as well as express their views better as well as participate actively in literacy classes, if the instruction is carried out in their working language.'

Many European and North American teachers of language and literacy have also held to these ideas, but rarely, if ever, would they have been attached to such a process of language learning that has been so strategically concentrated, involved so many languages and taught so many people to read and write with so little in the way of professional resources as in the Ethiopian campaign. What of course Ethiopia has, which most other educational projects do not have, are mass motivation and mobilisation, and a high degree of popular democratic energy and organisation at every level of the execution of its literacy campaign.

Dialects: A Continuing Issue

Yet the awesome complexities facing literacy educators within the network of so many languages in Ethiopia continue to raise very sensitive problems. Many of these concern the weighty issues of dialect. In his detailed study, entitled *Some Impacts of Dialectal Differences on the National Literacy Campaign of Ethiopia*, Mammo Kebbede Shenkut gives some startling examples of the difficulties thrown up by dialect differences to literacy teachers in Ethiopia who are using the main mother tongues as languages of instruction. The under–developed transport system that exists within the country and the barriers of terrain have often made communications within the country extremely problematic, creating isolated villages and homesteads and making conditions very conducive for the growth in language variation and dialect. In addition, the problems caused by dialect in the border areas of Ethiopia have themselves been further complicated by a confusion of written forms – particularly when the peoples are nomadic and continually cross and re–cross national boundaries. For example, the Somaligna–speaking people of Hararge region in Ethiopia learn their language using the Ethiopic syllabary: Somalis learning the same language in literacy classes in Somalia across the border use the Latin or European alphabet.

Dialects, indeed languages, can vary from village to village, as well as district to district and region to region. In Sidamo region, for example, six major languages are used within the literacy campaign, and while in Awassa, the regional capital, I was shown the same poster in use in the region overprinted in Amharic, Oromigna, Somaligna, Wolayitigna, Sidamigna and Gedeogna. The logistical problems teaching literacy in such a context are, of course, intense and complex. Oromigna, for example, is spoken by many millions of Ethiopians stretching through ten regions and has not surprisingly developed wide–ranging regional dialects and several local varieties. This has produced marked phonological differences within the language as well as semantic differences. For example, in the Harar dialect of Oromigna, 'bukkie' means 'hermaphrodite', yet in the Shewa dialect it signifies 'side by side'. The word 'ulfessu' in Harar means 'to impregnate', while in Shewa it can mean 'to respect'. One dialectal meaning of the Gedeogna word 'tonbba' means 'tobacco', another is 'vagina'. Such variations of course can create many social as well as educational confusions and problems for teachers and students.

Before the literacy campaign took grip on Ethiopia's languages, there was no standard dialect in any of the languages of nationality, with the exception of Amharic. In order to remedy this, nationality language committees were established for each of the other fourteen languages employed in the campaign, ensuring that these structures would include representation from all major dialect speakers. The committees were responsible for preparing the texts for use in the campaign, and translating them from the originals in Amharic into the nationality languages, ensuring that dialect factors were fully taken into account. From this stage the text passes to the editing sub–committees which check and finalise the texts — and to the graphic artists, who are guided by the sub–committee in the cultural traditions, clothing, instruments and utensils used by the people speaking the particular languages in their illustrations to the texts and primers.

Even with all this care and scrupulous organisation, the problems of dialect have continually re–surfaced for those involved in the campaign, and sometimes economic losses have been caused when students in particular districts have rejected their primers and texts because of dialect differences. Mammo Kebbede Shenkut recalls a number of concrete instances of this happening. He remembers, for example, when he went to evaluate the programme in the regions of Bale, Sidamo and Gamo Gofa:

> Lots of Oromigna primers and readers were piled up in the stores and literacy centres in Bale Region and in Gardula province of Gamo Gofa. When the responsible local officials were asked why it was so, their answer was that the adults did not want to use them on the pretext that they were not prepared in 'their' language.
>
> A similar example comes form the Asawurta elders in Eritrea. Officially Asawurta is a dialect of Saho. Some Asawurtas claim, however, that their language is Asawurta and is different from Saho. A few years ago some elders prepared a syllabary chart and a primer in what they called 'Asawurtigna' and approached the National Literacy Campaign Co–ordinating Office to get the materials printed. It was not accepted however on the grounds that it was a dialect of one of the languages being already used for literacy. Furthermore the NLCCC was not mandated to prepare literacy materials in more than fifteen languages. Even if there was a mandate, a thorough study from various angles would be needed to decide the order of priority of languages and weigh this against the resources.

Such dissatisfaction meant that many of the Asawurtas retained a negative attitude to the Saho primers. Then, in the south of the country, a whole truckful of Somaligna primers were sent back to the campaign headquarters in Addis Ababa by the Hararge Committee, who said that they could not make use of them as they did not authentically express their dialect.

Similar questions were asked by trainers in the Gamo Gofa region in 1985. 'Why should the Gamos and the Gofas use the literacy books printed in Wolayitigna?' Mammo Kebbede Shenkut tells us what happened:

> The answer given was that because they are dialects of Wolayitigna. When those who asked why Wolayitigna should be used for the Gamos and the Gofas, were themselves asked whether or not they understood the language in which the teaching materials were prepared, their response was that they understood it well, but that since the cover title says 'Wolayitigna', it should be given to the Wolayitas.
>
> This simply means that they do not mind the content and the language in which the content is expressed. But they want the cover title to read 'Gomogna', etc. Had there been a comprehensive name accepted by all, there would not have been any problem with the teaching materials as they are.

The multiplicity of languages and dialects throughout Ethiopia has always been a vital factor in its cultural wealth and uniqueness. The National Literacy Campaign is proving to be both a guardian and guarantor of the diversity of this invaluable inheritance, while also ensuring that the entirety of the country pulls together and unifies its huge language resources, and extracts the maximum energy and coherence from them. For language is the route towards development and progress as well as the vehicle of history and identity. A measure of the achievement of the National Literacy Campaign is that it is managing to secure progress in all these emphases in the midst of massive material pressures, shortages and constraints.

Notes

1. *Every Ethiopian Will Be Literate and Remain Literate*: The National Literacy Campaign Co–ordinating Committee: Addis Ababa, 1984.

2. 'The Constitution of the People's Democratic Republic of Ethiopia': Addis Ababa, 1987.

3. *Literacy in Ethiopia: At the Gateway of Light*: Interview with Neway Wolde Sadik: City of Sheffield Education Department, 1986. Also see Wolde Sadik, N, *National Literacy Campaign with Reference to the Experience of Ethiopia*, A paper for Kitwe (Zambia) Seminar, Addis Ababa, 1985.

4. Interview with Mammo Kebbede Shenkut by author, Addis Ababa, October 1988.

5. Bhola, H.S. *Campaigning For Literacy*: International Council for Adult Education: 1981.

6. Mammo Kebbebe Shenkut, *Some Impacts of Dialectal Differences of the National Literacy Campaign of Ethiopia*: Addis Ababa,1988.

Corrugated iron literacy poster at Ade Aro Village

4.
'LET EVERYBODY LEARN!': THE BEGINNINGS OF THE CAMPAIGN

Formal education in Ethiopia began as a direct response to the threat from the colonial powers and their more advanced technology, which had brought so much imperial domination and damage to the peoples of Africa during the nineteenth century. After his victory over these forces at Adwa in 1896, Menelik showed the reforming side of his autocracy when he declared that 'our young men must be educated', and despatched a small number of them to other countries for schooling and training. By 1908, the first foundations of a very limited school system were being born, as the emperor made it quite clear that at least a proportion of Ethiopians must be educated, in order to 'ensure our peace, reconstruct our country, to enable it to exist as a great nation in the face of the European powers.'[1]

These modest initiatives towards state education had produced only 21 government schools by 1935, and after the expulsion of the Italian invaders a few more schools were established, so that Haile Selassie's feudal regime would have an educational strata of loyal supporters in order to maintain and consolidate the Empire's state bureaucracy and state power.

A Policy of Parsimony

There was much talk about the importance of education and literacy for the people within the elite circles around the Emperor, but very little commitment to allocate either money or resources. In 1952 the Ministry of Education produced an impressive–sounding 'Ten Year Plan for the Controlled Expansion of Ethiopian Education', advocating a system of state education that would promote mass literacy and ensure that all Ethiopians would 'live better, healthier and productive lives'. Concretely, this was revealed as cosmetic rhetoric when the proposed '35 schools a year' plan was abandoned in 1964.

In 1955 the first adult education and literacy initiative was taken by the regime with the Emperor's 'Literacy Proclamation', which again was words without resources. It showed grotesque cynicism towards the vast majority of Ethiopian people who were struggling against the poverty and backwardness which feudal rule had brought them, to tell all illiterate individuals to employ 'a private teacher in his respective village or district', so that they could learn Amharic, the one language acceptable to the imperial government. And this for a people whose gross domestic product per capita for 1973 was 161 Birr (or $77, in 1960 prices). They were to go out on the education market and try to 'buy' literacy education!

The first sign of any real state resources developing around the crying need for literacy arrived in 1960 with a consortium of government, non–government and religious agencies – including the Ministry of Education, the Ethiopian Orthodox Church, the Ethiopian Women's Welfare Organisation, the Police Force and the University Students Association. In 1962 this developed into a 'voluntary' body, the 'National Literacy Campaign Organisation', with the Emperor as 'Patron', the Crown Prince as 'Honorary President' and with the Patriarch of the Orthodox Church and the Prime Minister as 'Honorary Members'. However all this prestige at the top was not matched with resources at the bottom, and by 1964 only 27,000 out of Ethiopia's nearly 40 million illiterate people had received any literacy instruction.

By 1967 a Division of Adult Education and Literacy had been finally established in the Ministry of Education, as a direct response to international exposure of the illiteracy rate of 93% within the country.

However, the new division was given a minimal budget and a staff of only five individuals, and proved to be little more than a token response to a situation of permanent educational crisis for the mass of the population. This mere gesture became even more tragically ironic when Ethiopian delegates to the Tehran Conference of 1965 organised by UNESCO had pledged that their government would commit major resources and do everything that they could to speedily eradicate illiteracy among the people!

It was ultimately through the intervention and support of UNESCO and the UNDP internally within Ethiopia that a pilot project called 'Work Oriented Adult Literacy' was pioneered in 1968.

This became the first seriously resourced attempt in the country to link literacy methods to development programmes and concentrated upon three rural areas and two urban contexts.

For the colleagues working in the Division of Adult Education, this pre–revolutionary period of such feeble state conviction towards literacy meant acute frustration, professional insult and often a sense of despair. Neway Wolde Sadik, who directed the Adult Education Department during this period, has described the parsimony of the regime:

> The meanest thing about the pre–revolution literacy programme was using only one language and two primers without follow–up books or functional materials to safeguard the neo–literates from elapsing into illiteracy. The only safety measure, of course, for those who could afford it, was attending very expensive evening classes, opened to exploit rather than impart knowledge and skills.

Out in the regions, the situation was even more dire: 'We would have just one single organiser for vast amounts of illiterate people'.

Illiteracy presented just one more dimension of the oppression and deprivation visited upon the Ethiopian people by the feudal elite. Yet it was a particularly onerous and significant one, and a facet of life which led directly to the boiling up of popular humiliation and rage, and the eventual overthrow of the system. As Neway Wolde Sadik asserts so emphatically:

> Ninety–three per cent of our people were blindfolded by illiteracy, and this was one of the causes for our revolution, one of the spurs that made them rise up against the imperial regime.[2]

The 1974 Revolution

The frivolous and piecemeal approaches made by the Haile Selassie government would never seriously challenge illiteracy in Ethiopia. Only a wholehearted and determined campaigning strategy, mobilising all sections and democratic organs of the society could achieve that.

The momentous events of February 1974 marked the turning point for the illiterate millions of the country, and significantly, teachers and students themselves – who were to become the future literacy campaigners – had been an integral part of the forces that brought the regime down. They had been in the forefront of demonstrations in Addis Ababa, demanding the transformation of education across the nation, and carried their placards side by side with those of the workers and peasants, which proclaimed 'Land to the Tillers'. For it was clear that a change towards literacy and education for all could only be achieved through a radical rupture with everything from the past.

Thus education for the 90% of Ethiopians who depended on the land had to depend on land reform. If the motor of education is motivation, and the assurance that change and the betterment of life will result from the act of learning, the land had to be its source. In March 1985, when the revolutionary government, under the leadership of the Provisional Military Administrative Council (PMAC) abolished feudal relations and land tenure arrangements, and created the conditions of huge economic and political progress for the peasantry, suddenly there was a reason for study, a cause for the acquisition of new skills and knowledge. The old system, which meant that peasants had to render up to three quarters of their produce to the landlords, was ended in a stroke. All rural land was nationalised and private ownership abolished. Leasing of land and the hiring of labour to cultivate land was banned and a limit of ten hectares was placed on the amount of land a single peasant could hold. This single drastic step created entirely new conditions for the furtherance of mass education in Ethiopia and was a pre–requisite for an effective, campaigning approach to literacy.

In addition, urban lands and extra houses were also nationalised, together with factories, bank and insurance companies — and schools were moved from the private domain and brought under the control of the state and the people. Suddenly, education became a possibility for all, and as a slogan later was to proclaim 'Education is a right, but literacy is a must!'.

But it was also the formation of new and entirely original models of mass organisation and mobilization that created the infrastructures on which genuinely popular educational initiatives could be founded.

Administratively, Ethiopia is divided into 14 regions (plus one portal administrative province, Assab, and the capital, Addis Ababa.) There is a further division of administrative units into 106 Awrajas or provinces, and these break down into 594 Weredas, or districts. But in addition to this network, the revolution took decisive steps to create further structures in which the people themselves could provide the revolution's driving force. Throughout the cities Kebeles, or urban–dwellers associations were formed at the neighbourhood level, and within the villages and rural areas

Gebere Maheber, or peasants' associations, become the main vehicles for mass participation in all the programmes brought by the revolution. Alongside these novel and locally elected organs, mass organisations of youth (REYA) and women (REWA) were formed, with branches in every urban and rural location, and new impetus was given to industrial workplaces with the growth of a new and vibrant trade union movement.

These organisations were to be the delivery agencies and support structures for the many new services the revolution would bring. And central to their development, and to the eventual success of the programme itself, was the literacy campaign.

The First Steps Towards Mass Literacy

By December 1974, nine months after the eruption of revolution, nearly 60,000 young people, in the main secondary schools and university students, plus large numbers of teachers, formed the major cohort of the 'National Work Campaign for Development through Co–operation'. This was to become an important dress rehearsal for the even more massive organisational effort which was later to be invested in the literacy campaign. The First 'Zemecha', as the 1974 initiative was called, involved the young people and members of the armed forces spending two years in the rural areas where their brigades helped in the reorganisation of peasant life and the formation of the peasants associations. While engaged in this work of social reconstruction, they also managed to register over three quarters of a million people for literacy work, 160,000 of whom completed their courses. During this prototypal exercise, there was a practical opportunity to pilot new teaching materials and approaches to learning, many of which were to be applied and consolidated during the years of the literacy campaign.

As a part of 1976 Programme of the National Democratic Revolution, the commitment towards popular education and mass literacy was made explicit: 'There will be an educational programme that will provide free education, step by step, to the broad masses... All necessary measures to eliminate illiteracy will be undertaken'. Then in June 1979 the government made public that during the following month the National Literacy Campaign would be launched. At a large meeting held at the National Theatre in Addis Ababa, foreign diplomats and ambassadors were informed of the massive organisational nature of the enterprise, and an appeal went out to all those present for material assistance, from their governments.

Objectives

The five years between the outbreak of the revolution and the beginning of the campaign had been crucial for any success it might achieve. It would have been impossible to have launched directly into mass literacy work without the structures to support and deliver it. Those five years had provided those necessary mass structures which could effectively institutionalise the campaign and mobilise all its participants – including learners, teachers, administrators and fund–raisers. But even more fundamentally they had been years during which the revolutionary commitment of Ethiopia's new government had been decisive. The political determination to defeat all manifestations of feudal backwardness was being expressed right across the nation.

As Bhola has written, 'without the clear expression of the political will by a society's power holders, a successful mass literacy campaign is most improbable'.[3] Ethiopia's new government had given notice of that will, and the mass organisations were ready to conduct it.

The objectives of the campaign were established on both a short–term and long–term basis. The first priority was to attack illiteracy in the urban areas and clear it out of the cities: after this the concentration would shift to the countryside and the mass of the population within the peasantry. Literacy, in the words of Neway Wolde Sadik, was to become the means of the majority of Ethiopian people 'acquiring theoretical, scientific concepts and skills for effective participation in economic, social and political affairs'. This means that the literacy campaign also had clear economic objectives, as the new knowledge that formed the content of the curriculum would build obvious linkages between literacy and agricultural development in the rural areas, helping the students to become more productive farmers, more efficient cottage industrialists, more successful soil conservationists or irrigators of their own land. Literacy would also make its students more conscientious about the sanitation of their homes and the health of their families and unborn children, more determined to improve all aspects of their domestic and social conditions. Finally, literacy was to be the foundation for post–literacy and a lifetime of continuing education, to begin the process of educational development that would drag the country out of all aspects of its backwardness and create the conditions for its scientific and technological progress. And in doing this it would make its students fuller people, would expand their skills and ability to more fully express their humanity – whether this was reading, and replying to, a letter to a son or a mother who lived hundreds of miles away, abandoning the shame of a thumb–print for the pride of a signature, or reading the poetry and literature of their own people, and contributing to it in newspaper, debate or cultural event.

An All–inclusive Structure

A national literacy campaign cannot be expected to succeed unless it genuinely takes its form and structure from all the active energies and constituent parts of national life. It cannot simply be a marginalised section of a division within the Education Ministry. If it is going to benefit from, as well as in turn become the vehicle of, an intense national mobilization, its organising direction must include active representation from all sectors of society. That breadth of involvement makes the difference between a limited exercise in the gaps within existing educational provision — often the pattern of literacy approaches in a non–campaigning context — and a mass programme that touches all points of the life of the people, and draws them into its involvement and benefits.

In Ethiopia, the overarching and all–inclusive structure that led the campaign, took the form of the National Literacy Campaign Co–ordinating and Executive Committee (NLCCC).

This committee was chaired by the Minister of Education but was inter–ministerial in its composition, also including within its membership the heads of other development ministries such as Health, Agriculture, Communications and Transport, Housing, Culture and Sports — with the Ministry of Information also playing a vital cohering and publicising role. The NLCCC assembled 28 representatives from these ministries, from the mass organisations, from professional organisations and also from religious bodies and institutions – which included the Ethiopian Orthodox Church, the Catholic Church and representatives from Islamic groups. It was a body of enormous organisational breadth and profoundly tentacular in its ability to affect and be affected by, all strands of Ethiopian society. In this sense, it was an expression and paradigm of the national democratic revolution.

A similar structure to the national committee, again including representation from all sectors, was established in each region, then again in each Awraja, and yet again in each Wereda. Finally, each Kebele and local peasants association also developed a co–ordinating and executive committee on the same pattern, so that from the national level, right down to the neighbourhood and village level, the direction and implementation of the campaign had the broadest possible cross–social involvement and support, and the committed participation of all progressive sections of social and institutional life. The Adult Education departments in the Ministry of Education and in the regional educational offices respectively, functioned as the administrative offices of the campaign, which was financed from government funds and budgeted for annually on the basis of the unit cost of each student. Fundamental resources like textbooks, charts, pens and pencils (when available from foreign donors), paper, schools' premises and the training of campaigners were all the budgetary responsibility of the government, yet the role of financial and material assistance from fundraising efforts internally to Ethiopia and internationally, was to become hugely important. In this, the campaign received a specially helpful boost when in June 1981 UNESCO made a worldwide appeal for resources. However, contributions from the Ethiopian public continued to be a vital source of funding, and it was the responsibility of the communities — co–ordinated by their Kebeles — to build literacy centres.

Each level of Co–ordinating and Executive Committee, from the national committee down to the local level, split its practical tasks into four sections, each to be handled by a further committee. This meant that each specific task was set out, carried out and monitored by one or other of these four executive arms. They are:

(i) Educational Materials Procurement and Distribution Committee;

(ii) Recruitment, Training and Placement Committee;

(iii) Propaganda and Aid Co–ordinating Committee;

(iv) Data Collection, Supervision and Certification Committee.

This organisational model was both simple and sophisticated. It exploited the already existing social and mobilizational infrastructures that the revolution had brought into existence, whilst also creating a multi–level fabric of implementation which assured an impressive breadth of mass participation at the most local level. As a model it was entirely Ethiopian: there was no way that any other existing literacy campaign structure could be simply imported and applied to the Ethiopian reality. It was a mode of organisation that had grown organically out of both the peculiar history of adult education in the country, and the unique organs of people's power and mobilization that had grown through the first five years of the Ethiopian Revolution.

A Compulsory Programme

Another characteristic that gave the campaign a certain uniqueness was its compulsory aspect. And yet it was a compulsion that could not have possibly worked without a national and popular willingness to co–operate with it. Compulsory education for children is an absolutely accepted right all over the world: yet compulsory literacy for all illiterate people between the ages of eight and forty–nine is not something with which many nations are familiar. Having been deprived of education for so many centuries and generations, the democratic imperative of the Ethiopian Revolution was not simply to be able to offer education to all, it was to ensure literacy for all. The element of compulsion too, was not so much directed towards the actual literacy students, but towards the elements within the society who had sought to erect barriers to their educational advancement. Thus, for example, in situations where employers might use their power or leverage over their employees, householders over their domestic servants or husbands or fathers over their wives and daughters – then the factor of compulsion was necessary, and the Kebeles or branches of the trade unions, peasant associations or REWA could invoke it on behalf of their members against those forces or individuals that were denying them the opportunity of literacy, self–development and equality.

Often employers, for example, might find it awkward if literacy classes were held at particular times of the day but they had to agree to their employees' release. There had to be wide flexibility in the timing of classes, depending upon the availability of light, the work patterns of the men and women students and the times when the particular venues were free. Many women found the hours of three in the afternoon until six most convenient, as by that time they had completed their housework, baked, made the family's injera and sauce and done their various other tasks. For men of the rural areas, their times of study were often dictated by weather conditions and the particular crops they were farming. Many preferred the early morning period between six and eight, particularly if they were using school premises which would be taken over by school students at eight o'clock. Others preferred to work in the fields during the cooler early morning period, and then to study in the late afternoon. Sometimes the time of the classes meant men and women studied together, other times they would be in separate groups. But at whatever time had been arranged, attendance was necessary, and representatives of the mass organisations would be around very quickly to remind any erring employer or father of his obligations to the literacy students, and to the overall development of the country.

The First 'Rounds'

Initial planning of the campaign set ambitious targets of eradicating illiteracy from all urban areas by 1982, and from rural regions by 1987. The latter date was fairly quickly revised and re–set for 1990. The campaign was organised in two four month 'rounds' every twelve months. In each year, the first round seeks to register and teach all those in the community who are illiterate: the second is regarded as a 'mop–up' and remedial round which reaches all those who were not included in, or who failed the first round. During this second round the new literates immediately move on to post–literacy classes, in order to prevent any relapse back towards illiteracy.

The response to the first rounds was massive and far in excess of anything either expected or planned for. The campaign was initially set up for 1.3 million students in the first round and one million in the third. In fact, there was a flood of enthusiasm: 6.2 million Ethiopians registered for the first round and 2 million more in the third. 34,599 literacy centres were quickly prepared and 241,143 instructors made up of teachers, students, soldiers, civil servants and factory workers were intensively trained for a week in order to service this huge cohort.

'Every place is a class for illiterates', proclaimed the slogan, as teaching venues sprang up in schools, church compounds, private houses, mosques, community centres and 'liquor houses'. As the entire country mobilized itself for this war on backwardness, slogans appeared on walls, trees, buildings and fences: 'We pledge to eradicate illiteracy by teaching and learning', 'Let the educated teach and the uneducated learn', 'Age is no barrier to education!', 'Literacy is part and parcel of the cultural revolution!', 'The curtain of ignorance will be torn asunder!', and 'Let everybody learn!'. Looking back to the drama of the first round, Neway Wolde Sadik remembers well the intensity and excitement of the mass activity.

> This was fantastic for us, but it became a very difficult situation for us to manage alone in the Ministry of Education. So

> other ministries and also some religious bodies and state-run agencies helped us, and with the help of the personnel and infrastructures of all those organisations – and also using the activity and enthusiasm of the teachers – we embarked upon the campaign, even though we had such a serious shortage of materials, alphabet charts and text books. So we had to use our own means and improvise. For example we took dry cell batteries and ground them down to black powder and used it as charcoal, then turned it into paint to make blackboards of our white walls. We used old sacks to make our alphabet charts and old X–ray films were used for cut–out letters for the charts and teaching aids. We operated on a shift system — often with forty adults in a morning class and fifty more in the afternoon, all using the same charts.[4]

The sense of consternation and surprise that shook the campaign organisers in no way undermined the progress of the campaign. They could deal with it! Despite the massive and unexpected pressure on resources, books, charts and instructors, the campaign continued, swollen by millions, and managed to steady itself through its own extraordinary powers of inventiveness and improvisation. As the Secretary of the Executive Committee later described:

> All the materials we had we gave out, and then we appealed to all those literate to teach with whatever they had available. They wrote alphabets on pieces of cloth, mats, rocks and the sides of tanks. In this way we kept them all in the programme.

Such a hurricane of activity was bound to have its casualties, and nearly two and a half million of those who registered for the first round dropped out before it was completed. This meant that Round Two, the 'mop up' and remedial round was also going to be an epic episode. The entire country became a factory of educational aids and materials as flash cards, cut–out letters, wall charts and blackboards were being manufactured in schools, literacy centres and skills training centres in all the regions. The campaign was showing its stamina and its ability to deal with the unexpected, even if it came in the form of extra millions of eager students. It was discovering its own logistics and mechanisms to deal with the colossal nature of what it had set out to remedy.

In this way began an epic education process that was to galvanise an entire people into learning and teaching, and in doing so consolidate the mass popular democracy which was the life–blood of their revolution. It was the working out in educational energy of the words spoken by Mengistu Haile Mariam during his May Day speech of 1980:

> In order to grasp the laws of nature, to forestall its wrath, and to march forward continuously towards prosperity, our starting point is the liberation of the broad masses from illiteracy.

Notes

1. Again in writing this chapter, I am particulary indebted to information gleaned from:
   Every Ethiopian Will be Literate and Remain Literate:
   The National Literacy Campaign Coordinating Committee, Addis Ababa, 1984 and *National Literacy Campaign with Reference to the Experience of Ethiopia*: Neway Wolde Sadik: Addis Ababa, 1985
2. *Literacy in Ethiopia: At the Gateway of Light*: Neway Wolde Sadik and Chris Searle: Sheffield 1985
3. Bhola, H.S.: *Campaigning for Literacy*, International Council for Adult Education: 1981
4. Wolde Sadik/Searle: 1985

5.
THE YOUTH GALVANISED

There is a wholesale reversal of the roles of generations happening now in Ethiopia through the National Literacy Campaign. We in Europe, who are accustomed to teachers being at least of adult and often of mature years, and students being young and inexperienced in life, may find it difficult to fully understand the identities of, and the relationship between the teachers and the learners in Ethiopia. But what is clear is that without the full and committed involvement of the organised youth, the campaign was never going to be successful and there would never be enough instructors to hold the fabric of teaching together. For it is the young people of Ethiopia who have provided the essential fuel for the campaign with their own enormous teaching impetus, and the improvised genius of their practical pedagogy. These are teachers who plunged themselves into the most challenging classroom work after just over one week's training and with few pre–made teaching resources. In their work is the fulfilment of Bhola's moving declaration about the essential driving force of popular mobilization:

> The sheer common sense of practitioners and their ability to learn from their own experiences has succeeded where prestigious groups of linguists, psychologists and pedagogues have stumbled ... Mobilization in its essential essence is a marriage of Utopian imagination and practical strategy, of emotion and intellect. It is a belief in the possibility of success in actualizing a new social order. It is discovering the resources we never thought we had. It is putting old things to new uses. It is a declaration of business unusual. It is rising against all odds. It is to change adversity to advantage. No mass literacy can succeed without effective mobilization.

Secondary School: Preparing For Democracy

It is an obligation for all secondary school students to make their vital contribution to the literacy campaign at the end of their year of twelfth grade. The last duty of their school life is to spend their final summer vacation period in four months of literacy work, usually in a rural part of their own province or language zone where there is a need for instructors to be brought in. Literacy tasks are integral to their school career, and Grade 12 students are required to teach at least one round of the campaign, after which they are issued with a certificate of service. Thus literacy work is institutionalised within school life as a normal dimension of any student's work.

By the time in her school life when she comes to do her literacy service, an Ethiopian school student will have grown up within a system where democratic behaviour and involvement is a natural process. Every secondary school has a branch of the Revolutionary Ethiopian Youth Association (REYA), with its class representatives and officers elected annually by the student body. The branch is responsible to REYA structures at a higher level, and also to the School Committee, on which a REYA delegate sits as an elected member. The School Committee of eleven members has general control and oversight over the school, and is composed of representatives of local Kebeles or peasants associations, REYA and the teachers union. It elects its own Chairman, but the School Director is automatically both the Assistant Chair and Secretary. Thus the school is very much under the general direction of the local community, but with its administrative arm controlled by the state. This partnership is also expressed in the financing of schools, for while the Ministry of Education pays the teachers' salaries and provides the buildings, the cost of any materials, resources, educational equipment or the maintenance of furniture is the responsibility of the school. Every school must produce in order to survive and develop, and certainly this is happening very successfully in some schools. In Misrak Comprehensive High School in the east of Addis Ababa, for example, the school is producing high–quality metal stoves for the baking of injera, as well as making furniture for sale, and is selling grass from fields attached to the school to local livestock owners. So from life at school, young Ethiopians are apprenticed in the reality that educational development and economic development must go hand in hand if their country is going to achieve progress.

The school REYA branch itself has weighty responsibility, taking on the tasks of ensuring positive and democratic discipline within the school, mobilising the student body to take part in the school's productive and democratic life, and organising 'Labour Education' – which involves cleaning and maintaining the school and contributing to work in local factories or farms. But it is around the time of the summer school closure and the preparation for, and organistion of the literacy work from April to July, that the school REYA branch really moves into high momentum.

Training for the Campaigners

To cram what is necessary for a four month literacy course in just ten days, shows just how much the campaigner has to fall back on his own resources, creativity and power to improvise, while teaching in a village which is probably at a considerable distance from his urban home. In most cases students from the same school will go to literacy centres in the same Wereda, and will also be accompanied during those four months by their twelfth grade teacher. Some campaigners may already have had some instruction experience by taking evening literacy classes run by the Kebeles in their own neighbourhood. In fact, students in urban areas have a choice of literacy work as long as the literacy work continues in the cities: they can teach a sustained and complete evening course in a local neighbourhood as an alternative to the four month stint in the summer. But most campaigners are virtually green as teachers before they start their intensive week's training.

This includes short coaching courses on the principles of adult teaching and learning, the preparation of teaching aids from local materials, the construction of tests and the supervision of examinations and simple record keeping. Briefings are also given on participation in community development, how to clean and keep spring water and how to use dry–pit latrines, and how to maximise local and community 'know–how'.

Another vital area of training is the brief tuition in Adult Psychology. Whatever the students do, they are told they must always show a profound respect, consideration and politeness to students who are almost all going to be older than them, many of whom are the age of their parents and grandparents. Family life in Ethiopia is imbued with love and respect for elders, but young, urban, educated people who have the authority of an education over illiterate country people, could easily slip towards arrogance and superior airs. So they are told to refer to older students as 'Abbabba' (father) or 'Immamma' (mother), never simply as 'you'. They are advised to use expressions like 'Gashe' for an elderly man or 'Etiyye' for a woman of mature years. The objective is always to secure good and respectful relationships between the generations. An instructor who is continually disrespectful to an elderly student risks being expelled from the programme and losing his opportunity of gaining his certificates.

I asked Yohannes Beraki, a young Addis Ababa school director, about the attitude of his students to the tasks of literacy. Did they feel they were an imposition? As city dwellers did they feel alienated or threatened by four months in the countryside? Did they see the campaign work as an interruption to their education?

> They are positively glad to serve in the rural areas, they look forward to it. In Ethiopia now our mass media bring the good and positive aspects of rural life to our youth – the music, the dancing, the handicrafts, the clothes, the culture. The alienation between town and country was much more a feature of life before the revolution.
>
> In those days, a lucky student might go to university from a minority language group for example, and would change his name to disguise his family origin. Now, with the literacy campaign such students have a new pride in their language and all aspects of their nationality. Similarly, students in those times were often ashamed of their peasant fathers, and would hide the fact, saying that their fathers were 'big men'. Now we see right through the school a tremendous pride in peasant backgrounds and origins. Our students have experienced peasant life and hospitality, eaten their foods, learned their music and dances.
>
> And remember too, that in order to be a teacher in the cities — and in particular in Addis Ababa, it is necessary to have taught in the rural areas and taken part in the activities of rural production. I myself taught for several years in Gambela before I was appointed here. So all our teachers have blisters on their hands and are proud of it! They tell the students about the importance and the satisfaction of having had experience in the villages.

The Impact of REYA

As the organised expression of the young people of Ethiopia, REYA's contribution to the literacy campaign has been immense. During the years since its formation in 1980, when it was established out of existing student councils and religious youth organisations, the literacy campaign has been its main social activity.

Starting from a membership level of three million, it saw its main functions as the mobilisation of youth in the tasks of building socialism in and disseminating Marxist ideas in Ethiopia, and in seeking to encourage a positive attitude towards work and education. But it was by launching itself confidently into the literacy work that its intentions and plans were put to practical test.

REYA's first important contribution to the campaign was to take much of the responsibility in identifying its potential students. Sensitivities and complexes that existed between people of different language and ethnic groups in Ethiopia, made the process of identification a particularly difficult one. But on top of this task was the work which needed to be done with the youth themselves, in order to explain to them and convince them that it was only they who could form the massive teaching force that was needed if the campaign was to be able to achieve success. Who among the youth could run the first classes and thus become exemplary to thousands of others? Who were the most mature and likely to be most skillful at approaching adults and encouraging them to form a part of the first cohort of literacy students? These were important questions, and it was REYA which set out to find the practical answers.

The first round of the programme, being restricted to the urban areas, meant that the key local organs of mobilization were the Kebeles. So a strong working alliance developed between school REYA branches and the Kebeles, firstly in the work of identifying teachers and teaching venues. The targeted potential teachers were twelfth grade students, existing school teachers and literate young workers. As the latter were already often involved in working right through the day, it was soon found that the bulk of the literacy work fell upon the twelfth grade students.

The Process of Identification

While REYA at all times emphasised the need for careful sensitivity when its members set out to identify the first literacy students, it also stressed that within communities there must be no pretence and no secrets about the truth of illiteracy. With posters and slogans becoming internalised across the nation, and images and radio waves reminding all Ethiopians that 'Illiteracy keeps us in the dark' or that 'Illiteracy is the arch–enemy of economic development', or showing very graphically a blindfolded man stumbling across a terrain crossed with ravines and chasms, the message that illiteracy was more than a handicap, but a huge stumbling block to personal and national progress was penetrating the consciousness of all. It was in this context that REYA members set out upon their tasks of identification, with their own members who were in need of literacy becoming the first students and playing an exemplary role to other citizens.

Door Sticker used to indicate that a household is now free of illiteracy

Together with Kebele members they went on a house–to–house survey, establishing exactly who was illiterate in each household with personal interviews with the 'head' of the house and the rest of the family. The need for dialogue, for convincing potential students through measured discussion and principled debate was always stressed, and agreement that someone in the household was in need of literacy instruction was marked by attaching a black sticker to the door of the house. This sticker comprised a pen pointing diagonally across the sheet, behind the symbol of the literacy campaign – which itself depicted a student of the campaign writing at a desk and the rays of sun over his head shining from the word 'knowledge'. Across the pen on the sticker was printed: 'This house is not free of illiteracy', and below this 'Do not detach this until this house is free of illiteracy'. On each side of the pen were slogans, above was: 'We shall tear down the curtain of illiteracy through out struggle', and below: 'I pledge to eradicate illiteracy from my house', with a space for a signature beneath. So even to sign the statement, the householder may have needed to learn to write his signature. The sticker was headed by whatever regional or district Literacy Campaign Co–ordinating Committee was the organising agency for that household.

The objective was always that the householder himself would attach the sticker and take responsibility for it. It would never be attached using any form of coercion. If a householder was reluctant to allow any member of the family to go to literacy classes, or unwilling to attach a sticker, the only expedient to be used was persuasion and rational argument, and for this to be effective it might take several visits by Kebele representatives or members of REYA. Then having attached the sticker and the illiterate family members having been registered as literacy students, there eventually came the occasion when the student became a literacy graduate and the black sticker would be replaced. This is a time of celebration in the household, and a sense of honour and achievement for all its members. A red sticker is placed over the black one. It has the same basic design, but across the pen this time is inscribed. 'This house is free from illiteracy!'. Above the pen is the name of the Kebele co–ordinating authorisation officer, and below the householder is invited to sign his name under the words: 'I confirm that there is no illiterate person in my house'. At the bottom of the sticker is the declaration 'We are free from illiteracy through our revolution!'.

Building A New Youth

In giving the youth of Ethiopia major new responsibilities and expectations, REYA has made a fundamental contribution to the development of the confidence and vision of the generation that must consolidate the gains made by the earlier generation of revolutionaries. The literacy campaign has been the main vehicle for steeling the youth and giving them the direct experience of being a part of practical innovation and country–wide mobilization. I asked Mengistu Edo, who is head of the Youth Participation Department of REYA, what he considered were the most positive features that had arisen from the participation of young Ethiopians in the literacy campaign — both for the youth and the success of the campaign itself.

Apart from learning how to set about planning and organising a mass programme, more than anything else our young people have learned the value of patience. Even though we had so much to achieve in such a short time, our people would not be rushed, they would not simply be herded into activities which they did not understand. So our young people needed to help them to understand, to persuade and convince them – and this all took patience and careful thought and planning. Their work in the process of identifying students for the classes, and showing them the advantages of literacy, taught them a great deal about how to work with people respectfully and patiently, and to base everything on dialogue. After all, they were talking to their neighbours, people in the same community.

Then in the rounds beginning from Round Three, when the campaign was extended into the rural areas, our young people had to prove themselves even more. Because of the unequal distribution of schools in Ethiopia and the fact that most of our schools had been established in urban areas, in many cases Awrajas in the countryside did not have available twelfth grade students to act as instructors. So if a province was not self–sufficient in potential literacy teachers, it needed to borrow them from another province which had speakers of their language. Many of our cities still have young people who speak the languages of the rural areas, because their parents may have moved from those areas in order to become workers in the cities. So the literacy campaign gave our young people the opportunity to regain connection with their family roots and culture, and to dismantle any barriers which may have been built between the people of our cities and rural areas.

So our young city people saw it as a real adventure to work in the country regions, a real discovery about themselves and their own people. It wasn't so much a case of meeting resistance to working there as having too many candidates! During those four months they found out so much, and had such a deep education. They came home with photographs, songs, proverbs, drawings and music – they had picked up the wisdom and culture of the rural people. The Addis Ababa students, for example, who went to teach in the Sidamo region came back to Addis proudly wearing the embroidered clothes of the region! And while they were teaching in the country areas, the students took the responsibility of establishing and building up the resources in the reading rooms, the mini–libraries in each village. So now they have returned they do not forget the situation of the villagers. They are collecting books and texts, and periodically sending them to the reading rooms, so that their ex–literacy students who are now in the post–literacy phase will always have fresh reading material and do not fall back to the dangers of relapse. And their experience in the villages and preparation of educational aids, local materials and themes, has enabled them to know the most suitable texts for their ex–students, and the kind of specific problems and everyday issues that they are facing in their lives.

All this work of connecting the cities with the countryside has helped our revolution establish the foundation of genuine equality between urban and rural life, and our young people, organised through REYA, have been the main catalysts of this through their hard work and all they have achieved in the literacy campaign.

Notes

1. Bhola H.S. *Campaigning For Literacy*, International Council for Adult Education, 1981.
2. Interview with Yohannes Beraki, Addis Ababa, October 1988.
3. Interview with Mengistu Edo, Addis Ababa, October 1988.

Literacy students of Boditi, Sidamo region

ውሃን ንጹሕ ማድረግ የሚቻለው እንዴት ነው?

ለመጠጥ ወይንም ለምግብ መሥሪያ አገልግሎት የሚውለውን ውሃ ሁሉ በማፍላት ንጹሕ ማድረግ ይቻላል ።

በአካባቢ ማግኘት የሚቻለውን ውሃ በማፍላት በውስጡ የሚገኙትን ጥቃቅን በሽታን አምጪ ነፍሳት ሁሉ ማጥፋትና ውሃውን ንጹሕ ማድረግ ይቻላል ።

ለመጠጥ የሚሆን ውሃ እስኪፍለቀለቅ ድረስ በንጹሕ ማሰሮ መፈላት አለበት ። ውኃን ማጥለል ለዐይን የሚታዩትን ነፍሳትና ሌላም ቆሻሻ ነገሮችን ይለያል ። ማፍላቱ ደግሞ በዐይን የማይታዩትን ጎጂ ነፍሳት ይገድላል ። የተፈላውን ውኃ በተፈላበት ዕቃ ከድኖ ማስቀመጥ ነው ።

Page from a literacy follow–up booklet on the boiling of drinking water.

6.
ORGANISING THE WORD

> Now our people are no longer frightened or shy of education, they see it as common and familiar to their lives. Education used to be far away, used to seem distant, but now it has come to the gates of our people. Now, they feel that to achieve literacy is to gain dignity and to be able to use that skill, there is a role for all our people in the democratic structures we are building, in particular the Peasants' and Urban Dwellers' associations. So our people feel like new men and new women with literacy. Because they can use their skills and serve their country and its people in new ways they feel they are at the gateway of light. It's a rebirth for our people, and that too is one of our slogans. And it means a new confidence in simple things too. Now they can tell if a bus is a number seven or a number eleven and where it is going. It unlocks their daily life and makes new meanings all the time.[1]

These words spoken by Neway Wolde Sadik show how a new confidence has broken out within the mass of the Ethiopian people, who even two decades ago had been bludgeoned into reticence by feudal institutions and oppression. But such confidence does not arise automatically from the joy of release from grim conditions, or from the simple knowledge that you now have a government which is on your side. It comes as the result of the hard daily tasks of organising, or generating collective activity and bringing new benefits to a long–downtrodden people. Literacy is perhaps the strongest example of such a benefit in Ethiopia today, and the reason why its delivery has been so effective is the force of the mass organisations that have been its vehicles. It takes courage enough to embark upon literacy if formal education has passed you by all your life, if you have been strapped to a plough or kept in a kitchen from your days of childhood. And it often needs the confidence born of union, of collective endeavour, to propel a man or woman towards the self–belief they need to pick up a pen or follow letters on a page.

From Kitchen to Literacy Class

Even amongst the very small 7% of the population who were literate before the onset of the literacy campaign, just over 2% were women. It was a symptom of a violent and overwhelming oppression of womanhood, and one which Ethiopian women saw very clearly as a badge of their degradation. Stifled in an endless domesticity, bonded to childbearing, having no opportunity to grasp even the most basic opportunity of formal education, it was not surprising that they nursed a yearning for literacy. So there was an obvious historical logic to why women formed the majority of the first cohort of students when Round One of the campaign began in 1979. As the millions of Ethiopians registered for classes in July of that year, it was found that 73% of the entrants were women. Not only that, women also played the role of 'persuaders' of their husbands, brothers, fathers and sons. Some men were even threatened with divorce if they refused to take advantage of the literacy campaign. Thus women, who as girls, only formed 34% of the primary school intake, were dominating adult education and widening the route for the millions of others that were to follow them in the later rounds – for women have always formed the majority of the student body through the whole progress of the campaign.

The grasp of literacy has meant that the narrow boundaries of life that enclosed Ethiopian women are being continually pushed back. Women selling their small piles of fruit and vegetables in the market of Addis Ababa read while they wait for custom, planning how their life may change as a result of literacy. Women moving with their family, their basic belongings and utensils from the drought–torn areas of the north to the fertile, re–settlement lands of the south–west, carry their literacy primers and practise their exercises at overnight shelters, envisioning a new life with the skills they will gain from study. Women in the villages of Sidamo region make mud bricks and build houses – a task always previously performed by men – having read and studied the methods in their textbooks.

In the city of Awassa, the regional capital of Sidamo, I visited a class of post–literacy students who had recently graduated from the campaign's nineteenth (beginners') round. They were all either housewives, house servants or barmaids, and they were being taught by a nineteen year old twelfth grade graduate, Zenebework Negussie, who was about to sit her university entrance examination. As they completed some cloze exercises and read practice texts about the prevention of malaria and the draining of pools of stagnant water, I asked them about how the achievement of literacy had changed the way in which they saw their own futures.

Twenty year old Konjit Kebede, a barmaid, remembered how many people in her neighbourhood used to fall sick when she was a young child, and saw how literacy was making her neighbours and herself much more aware of the causes of common diseases and how to prevent them. Her ambition was to leave her present work, study some courses in preventative medicine and try to find work somewhere in the medical field. She said she read continuously – even at work, if she found the opportunity. Her deskmate was Wagayehu Mola, who was also twenty and worked as a house servant in Awassa city. Her writing was full of confident flourishes, and she was clearly progressing well. Her objective was to continue her studying as far as she could go, with the intention of eventually qualifying as a kindergarten teacher. As only that year, an ex–illiterate of Awassa who had been a graduate of the First Round had just gained entry on a degree course at Addis Ababa University, her hopes were far from impossible. Sitting beside her was Almaz Basa, another house–servant of nineteen years. She told me that she did not find the literacy work difficult, and that she had a very good teacher who made the lessons seem easy. At work she often reads while she cooks the meals, and just as long as it has no negative effect on the quality of the meals, she said her employer does not object! She said she was determined to reach for more satisfying work, and wanted to carry on studying in post–literacy and beyond, in order to become a government worker. In each case, the young women were pleased and proud to leave their signatures with me, as an indication of their progress.[2]

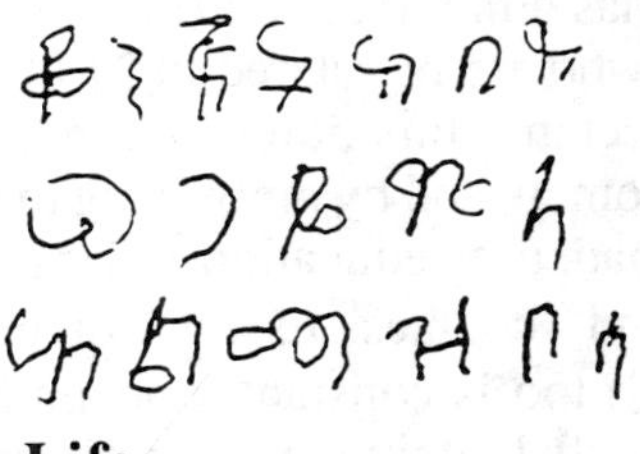

Reading Close to Life

Closely linked to the possibilities to expand life experiences through the achievement of literacy, women have also found the campaign very effective in improving daily life all around them. The subject matter of the primers, illustrations, exercises, sentence–building and post–literacy texts are all intimate to their living experience and face the problems with which they contend. This close connection with what they are reading is, of course, strengthened by its direct expression in their mother tongue. So the new words on the page go straight to the vital points in their life that they express with immediacy and frankness. As soon as the students are reading they are reading basic follow–up texts with such subjects as Clean Water and its Use, Care for Pregnant Women, Getting Rid of Household Pests and Soil and its Conservation. In Functional Reader 2 they go on to study Poultry Production, Child Care, A Balanced Diet and Home Improvement, with Childhood Diseases, Vaccination, Transmission of Diseases and Getting Rid of Trash and Waste in Reader 3 and Personal Hygiene, Vegetable Gardening, Storage of Food, Common Disease Prevention and Breast Milk in the fourth. Other readers take topics such as First Aid, Methods of Coffee Planting, Family Living and Cooperative Education. All these subjects have a stark and practical relevance to the daily lives of students. In every sense, the literacy campaign is not simply preparation for life, it is how to live life better, more securely and more productively.

The Dynamo of REWA

Just as REWA representatives sit on the National Coordinating committee of the Literacy Campaign, the local chair of REWA is automatically a member of every regional, Awraja or Wereda committee too. As Dereje Bekkele, the president of the Awassa Teachers Association declared, REWA's sucess has been 'to lead the women from their kitchens to go out to learn' — and in their millions.

REWA itself has a membership (on 1985 figures) of slightly over five million, who are registered in 21,000 branches throughout Ethiopia. Its declared function is to struggle towards equality for all Ethiopian women, and by mobilising them, continually raising confidence, broadening education and training through conferences, seminars and courses. Its own quarterly journal, *Addis Hiwot* ('New Life') too is constantly opening new opportunities for its members and challenging male domination in all areas of social, economic and political life. REWA plays particularly important functions in maintaining many of the infrastructures of the country's relief and rehabilitation programmes and also supporting the widows and families of those who have been killed in the secessionist wars of the north. But as with REYA, it is in the massive organisational tasks associated with the National Literacy Campaign that REWA has both proved itself and steeled itself.

The headquarters of REWA is the ex–residence of the last emperor's favoured son, a suburban mansion in Addis Ababa. In these elegant and transformed surroundings, I asked the Chair of the organisation, Asegedech Bezuneh, about the work of REWA in the literacy campaign.

> Women have always been close to the heart of the campaign. Our biggest problem, and also a very major contribution that we have made so far, is in childcare. We are committed to organising temporary day care facilities at all the literacy centres, while the women are at their classes – and we select experienced mothers, who are also already literate to do this work. We have found that where there is a day care centre at a literacy centre, it becomes a tremendous encouragement to potential women students and men too.
>
> REWA is represented at every level, on every committee, national and local, of the campaign,so we are completely integrated and involved in all aspects of its work. We were there right from the beginning. Despite so few of us being literate when the programme began, we managed to recruit 300,000 teachers for Round One, and some women kept coming back and taught two rounds a year for the first few years of the campaign.
>
> We also raised a lot of funds during that first part of the campaign, one and a half million Birr (approximately $750,000 US), from events like potluck lunches and bazaars. That money proved vital to tide the campaign over until we received international assistance. We also did a lot of agitational work, trying to persuade women to join the campaign – as though millions didn't need much persuading! We organised discussion forums, dramatic sketches which showed the terrible disadvantages of being illiterate, and told stories about women who didn't know the numbers of city buses and ended up at the wrong destinations. And once our women registered we organised prizes and awards for the most successful students and held emulation sessions where we gave out books, radios, scarves and furniture for our sisters who had done very well. We had special meals, with the most conscientious student sitting in a special seat as the guest of honour.
>
> Then we also put a lot of emphasis on the opening and maintaining of village reading centres. We raised donations, collected books and newspapers, and in places where reading

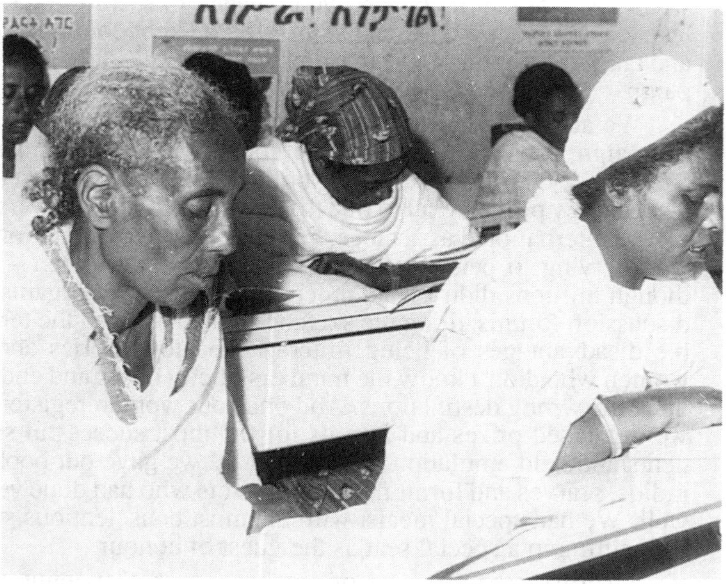

Ethiopian women comprise over 50% of the campaign's students

rooms hadn't yet been constructed we offered our own centres for use. All the time our members and officers are encouraging, persuading, urging women to attend day schools, evening classes, informal education sessions. And already half of our members who became literate in the early rounds of the programme, have reached twelfth grade.

All this activity in the campaign has helped to improve us as an organisation. It has made our organisation more efficient, has hugely improved our statistical work and markedly raised the confidence of our members. It also helped us to develop our cultural work. Now so many more of our members can read and write, so we have had more songs, chants, plays and poems and in our organisation alone, across the country we have organised 7,084 choirs!

The campaign has been like a spice to the women of Ethiopia, raising our courage and awareness. Our girls are much more confident, they're doing better at school, they're becoming lawyers and lecturers too. Before the revolution, even for the educated few, they would only ever become clerks, typists, teachers or nurses. Now we see women moving into skilled trades, becoming machine operators, tractor drivers, bus drivers, working on house and road construction — all this was unimaginable before 1974. The literacy campaign has helped to lift our women out of degradation and the squeezing limits that were put on their lives! And there is a massive change in attitudes happening too in Ethiopia. As men see this happening, they have to agree to send women to literacy centres and have to change the way they think and act too.

The campaign has had a strong effect on women in the lumpen areas of our society too. Although 85% of Ethiopian women are from peasant families, we still have 15% who live in the cities, and because of our severe inheritance of urban unemployment, some of them have been pulled towards prostitution. REWA organised studies of this situation in eleven of our cities, and we used the literacy campaign to try to rehabilitate these women. Many of them have now found proper jobs, or are being re–trained in our work–oriented literacy centres. We offered job priority to them, because as they were becoming literate they were saying to each other, and to REWA: 'Let's get out of this dirty job!'. Many such women are now married, and carry no stigma, and are working as tractor drivers, office workers or in cooperatives.

We are still struggling with the chauvinism of men at many levels. Some bureaucrats in offices, for example say women are incompetent workers. But we insist that REWA is not against men themselves, but against reactionary ideas, systems and practices which hamper the equality of women. But we know that we have the support of our party and government – and with vehicles like the Literacy Campaign to carry forward the strengths of our women, we know that such backwardness will eventually only be remnants of the past here in Ethiopia.

Letters in the Light

A regular feature in Ethiopia's daily paper, *New Era*, is a column called 'From Darkness to Light'. Here, every few days, letters are published, written by the newly–literate. They are short and uncomplicated, but often express in very plain and joyous words, the sensation of personal triumph over illiteracy and thus document pivotal moments in the lives of their writers.

Many of them are the work of women, and many pass on to other women the urge to learn to read and write. In this letter a daughter who is away from her family working in Addis Ababa, writes her first words to her mother, giving her the news of her progress:

> Dear Mother Almaz Mekbib
>
> How have you been feeling since we parted? I am very well, except that I am missing you.
>
> Dear mother, through the victory of our revolution I am now freed from illiteracy. See, I can write this letter to you! How about you, are you learning too?
>
> Please pass on my greetings to all the family. I would love to receive a letter from you too, in your own handwriting.
>
> Goodbye, until we write to each other again.
>
> Tsehaye Guche

And in another letter, written to her father, Abebech Argaw writes from Addis Ababa, asking him to share the joy of her literacy:

> I am well Daddy, but I also want to tell you that I am literate! I am so happy that I can read and write on my own. I hope you will be happy too that I have been so successful!

Men like Neway Wolde Sadik have seen on their pulses and been astonished by the transformation that Ethiopian women have brought to their own lives and that of their entire country through the power of words. They have grasped and held fast to the opportunities brought by the literacy campaign. Within a decade of literacy it is as if women have realised a whole new dimension of themselves which they are determined to consolidate and strengthen:

> Then there is the participation of women, who have been oppressed for generations. Traditionally their place has always been the home. They were not encouraged to come out of their homes to live a public life, to equate themselves with men, to work in offices, factories or to learn how to read and write. Now the revolution is creating equality between men and women as citizens, and the woman is no longer fixed in bondage. She is encouraged to come out of the home, organise and learn and gain what she has lost in the past. The formation of the Ethiopian Women's Association has helped to build this confidence, and is encouraging as many literate women as possible to teach their compatriots. Thus we have found that the registration of women in the literacy programme is in fact higher than men — and this is particularly marked in this year's figures (1986), where we have over eight million men and over nine million women registered. But because of the additional problems women face, their great tasks at home and their previous lack of contact with any form of formal education, we have seen that slightly fewer of them are passing their examinations. Remember she is still looking after the children, drawing water, cooking, tending the cattle, collecting firewood from a distance. She does all this, while the man may be ploughing for four hours, and then waiting for his wife to bring him his lunch in the fields! So the literacy campaign is helping to draw our women out of their homes and involve them in the programmes of our revolution, helping them to build that confidence among our women and telling them that the revolution is on their side. Of course, the materials and texts we produce for the campaign are telling the man that he must take part in the tasks of the house, must take equal responsibility for the children, must treat his wife with the respect due to an equal. These have provoked much self–criticism and self–awareness in a way that has not happened before. They are saying, "Who am I, and am I acting correctly?" Now it is not the women who feel shy and guilty, they are breaking into new confidence. It is the man now who is beginning to question and reflect about some of the ways in which he has been acting in the past and seeing how he must begin to make drastic changes in his life and way of living with women.[4]

Mural on a house in Ade Aro village

From the Plough to the Pen

Abdela Sonessa, the President of EPA, the Ethiopian Peasants Association, has had a remarkable educational career. A graduate of the literacy campaign himself from the western region of Illubabor, he is now the elected leader of Ethiopia's largest mass organisation, whose members constituted the largest part of the country's illiterates. As he declares quite unequivocally, 'unless we educate our peasantry, we cannot continue our struggle'.

When the literacy campaign spread from the urban to the rural areas of Ethiopia during its Third Round, it depended very largely upon EPA to agitate and mobilise the people, as well as to stimulate fund–raising and the contribution of vital materials for the campaign. The peasant families also provided accommodation in their houses, and food for the thousands of twelfth grade literacy instructors who arrived,virtually green to rural life, in their villages. They needed also to transport large quantities of paper, primers and other reading materials, blackboards and wall charts, and often cars were not available. And then at the end of the teaching round, there was also the construction and preparation of reading rooms and roadside reading booths — and the energy that needed to go into post–literacy work to ensure that there was no relapse among the newly–literate.

What had changed the habits of centuries for the Ethiopian peasantry? Steeped in superstition, individualism and feudal submissiveness, such collective endeavour would have been unthinkable before 1974. Yet with the transfer of land from the grip of private landlords to the people themselves, a new process of socialisation had begun. This first great move to liberate their labour was also a fundamental premise for the liberation of minds, and gave millions of peasants and their families a reason to learn. The land was now theirs, together with its produce. How could they grow more? How could they become better cultivators? How could they learn about new agricultural technology? How could they learn about fertilisers, more efficient strains of seed, how to protect their land from erosion, how to better conserve the water that only fell during a few weeks of the year? The answers were in the reading, in the learning. So the literacy campaign was there to make them into more efficient and productive farmers.

There is no doubt that the extension of formal education of rural children, and the opening of many new schools during the years after 1974, had a dramatic impact upon the consciousness of the peasantry. They saw their own children entering school — the first generation of their families ever to do so. The children brought their books and pens home and enthused to their parents about the value and excitement of learning. Some children began to teach their illiterate parents and grandparents who began at first hand to know and understand the advantages of education. Now there was a social context of organised education which had never existed before in the rural areas. Books were no longer strange, they were in the houses of millions of peasants, being read by their children every day. It was in the trail of this awakening to the mass education of children in country villages all over Ethiopia, that the literacy campaign arrived for their families.

'Let us have our school!'

'There are none so blessed as people educating each other', said Abdela Sonessa; 'and we are encouraged so much because of our success. We believe too, that for our pride we must overcome illiteracy.' I asked him to describe how important he considered the literacy campaign was for the millions of members of his organisation.

> The new culture of organised education in the rural areas had a dramatic effect on our peasant farmers and their families. As they built the new schoolhouses for their children, organised through their own local Peasants Associations, they began to ask each other 'Why not us, too? Our children have a school, they can read and write, they are learning so many new things. So why not us too? Let us have our school!'.
>
> What we have experienced in our country areas is, simply — change of life! With the growing literacy we have seen a new literate culture emerging. Our people writing letters, poems, making newspapers and leaflets, preparing the materials for reading rooms and display booths — and using their numeracy for keeping records, statistics, targets and figures. And this change of life has meant change in our surroundings too. As our people read the texts and act upon what they read, we look around us and see cleaner villages, better–built houses, less children sick and healthier bodies benefiting from balanced diets.
>
> In production too. You know that before the literacy campaign farmers in many parts of our country never used fertilisers. They used manure for fuel, not to enrich the soil. Now they use it as a fertiliser, along with the chemical fertilisers they get from the Ministry of Agriculture. They are reading about all this now – and also about selecting better stock, conserving soil and preventing the deterioration of their soil. They leave some land fallow now, and practise alternate farming, something they never did before. They are cultivating new vegetables too, like beetroot and sweet potatoes, and new fruits. For example apples were rarely grown in the north. That is quite common now, as there is a much greater knowledge about new methods of water conservation and irrigation. Our people are building dams with the knowledge built for them through the literacy campaign! Our books are written in such a way as to actually change the life of the peasant.

They are creating real innovations. For generations our traditions told us we must only plough using two oxen. Our donkeys were only used for transport. Now our people read about, and see in practice, single donkeys pulling ploughs quite efficiently. So they try it — it's easier and cheaper — and they are adopting it. The cycle of backwardness is broken in this way. Also pigs. It needs a change of culture for our people to eat pork, despite the fact that pigs are relatively easy to rear and the meat is nutritious – and it can be sold to the urban areas where it is very popular. People in Gojam never ate pork — they were fanatical about it. Now some cooperatives are beginning to raise pigs: that is a change in culture! Also people's health is improving because they fast less. And they eat more fish. We have many lakes in Ethiopia, huge lakes, but not much fishing has been done because the people, by tradition, ate little fish. Now they read about the goodness of fish in diet. So in Sidamo, Gonder, Gojam, and Gambela there is much more fish caught, sold and eaten.

In the areas of re–settlement the literacy campaign has played a very important role. As the people from the drought–affected areas move into the new villages, all social and educational facilities are waiting for them, organised by our Peasants' Associations. The literacy campaign helps understanding between the people who have come and the peoples who are already there. So this a vital force of social harmonisation between peoples of different nationalities.

You see, before the revolution and programmes like the literacy campaign, there was so much to divide our peoples internally in Ethiopia – whether it was religion, language, cultural rivalry, regional chauvinism, ethnicity. The revolution has made us struggle to create a new unity, and the literacy campaign has been so important because it has compacted us, made us feel and know that we are one people.[5]

Notes

1. *Literacy in Ethiopia: At the Gateway of Light*, Interview with Neway Wolde Sadik: Addis Ababa 1986.
2. Interviews in Awassa, Sidamo Region: November 1988.
3. Interview with Asegedech Bezuneh, Addis Ababa, November 1988.
4. *Literacy in Ethiopia: At the Gateway of Light*, as above.
5. Interview with Abdela Sonessa, Addis Ababa, November 1988.

A Sidamo farmer in a post–literacy class.

7.
A PEOPLE'S PEDAGOGY: THE CAMPAIGN IN SIDAMO

Sidamo is a large region in the south of Ethiopia. Its capital, Awassa is some 270 kilometres from Addis Ababa, and just over the boundary from the central province of Shewa. It borders Kenya to the south, the regions of Gamo Gofa and Kefa to the west and Bale to the east. It is the home of 3.7 million Ethiopians of ten nationalities, who speak six languages. As you drive south from Addis Ababa, the road towards Awassa runs through the huge rift valley, past large lakes like Langeno, Abayata with its teeming bird life, Shala and Abaya. The region is fertile and very productive. Large herds of cattle dominate the roadsides and huge expanses of the undulating lands are cultivated with maize and teff. It is an area rich in coffee cultivation, and there is also some extraction of gold. The landscape, particularly after the rains is green and lush, covering the hills, and cut by many river gorges. Across this countryside stretch lines of pylons, evidence of the electrification brought by the revolution, and new villages are growing everywhere, the result of the villagisation policy – each one offering to its people a health clinic, school and literacy centre.

In November 1988 I visited the region with a group of colleagues from the Division of Adult Education in Addis Ababa, in order to see the literacy campaign in action. What I saw and experienced left such a deep and lasting impression upon me as a teacher, that I have tried to set it down in the words that follow.

Briefing in Awassa

At a briefing given by the regional Co–ordinating and Executive Committee I began to understand the sheer size of the tasks of literacy that had been undertaken in Sidamo region alone since 1979. Whereas before the revolution only 4,396 people had become literate, since the onset of the campaign that number had increased to 1,687,896. The Sidamo colleagues described the two approaches to literacy that had been employed before 1979. Firstly there was the 'Orthodox' approach, when the churches and mosques gave a little literacy for religious study and worship, to a handful of regular worshippers. Secondly the 'Selective Intensive approach' was a method of 'picking out' particular regions and concentrating solely upon them while neglecting others. Now both these methods had been replaced by the 'Mass literacy' approach of the national campaign. The extent of this 'mass' programme can perhaps be gauged by considering the number of literacy books that had been given out throughout the campaign in the six languages of study in the region:

Amharic,	376,610
Wolayitigna,	227,108
Oromigna,	307,856
Sidamigna,	205,154
Gedeogna,	224,709
Somaligna,	29,935

Also 4,813 literacy centres had been in operation with 68,726 literacy teachers. 4,150 blackboards had been distributed with 4,171 gross of chalk plus thousands of blankets, shoes and field clothes for the campaigners. Out of all this had come 620,319 newly–literate people, many of whom had already registered for school, and 436,011 who were at present attending post–literacy classes.

So this was the context of the teaching and learning struggle and achievement that I found in Sidamo, as the committee set out to me what they saw as the priority objectives of their work. They had pared them down to four:

(1) To be able to read and write, and compute simple arithmetic in as short a time as possible.

(2) To apply literacy in every day activities so that the people can improve their living conditions.

(3) To apply literacy to acquire knowledge and skills for effective participation in economic, social and political affairs.

(4) To lay down the foundations for further education.

Again it was stressed to me how crucial to the campaign for literacy among the peasantry was the new situation of so many children of peasants being at school. With 841 new elementary schools in the region, 'every peasant has a child in school' and those children were the educational persuaders, and often the home tutors, of their parents.

A Teacher Speaks of Literacy

On the regional Coordinating Committee, teachers formed a strong contingent. The representatives of REWA and REYA, the Chief Education Officer representing the Ministry of Education and the Mayor of Awassa were all teachers. In addition Dereje Bekkele was on the committee as the representative of the local Teachers Association. It was from him that I learned about the role of teachers in the campaign and their work in mobilising their twelfth grade students in the tasks of literacy.

He explained how from their ninth grade onwards, Awassa school students would be expected to take on teaching tasks in their own neighbourhood, organised by the local Kebele. They would normally be fifteen to sixteen years of age at this stage in their schooling, and would clearly need a lot of help and support from their teachers and their REYA structures at school, to teach within their families. It is not until the end of the twelfth grade that they take on the obligatory literacy instruction work outside of their Kebele, or in more distant parts of their Awraja or region. For this work, of course, they must speak the language of the particular village to which they are assigned – and the process of organising this when there are six languages at work in the region is often complicated.

Dereje Bekkele spoke about the contribution of the teachers with pride and eloquence: 'To be a teacher in Ethiopia', he declared, 'is to be at the forefront of struggle and change'.

> Our teachers were exploited too during the time of the old regime, and many of them were dismissed from their posts or gave their lives because they strove to change the minds of their students, make them more conscious, and teach them ideas of struggle and freedom. And we have been organised for a long time. 1988 is the fortieth anniversary of our Teachers' Association. In 1974 we were side by side with our students and the peasants in the demonstrations which brought down the regime in Addis Ababa, just as we are side by side with them now in the work we do together in the Literacy Campaign.
>
> Our teachers rallied to the revolution, and played a major part in mobilising our people. When the revolution broke out 1974 we had 7,330 members of our Teachers' Association in Sidamo and of that number 4,200 were elected to hold office in the mass organisations like REWA and REYA. That's how committed our teachers are to see our country progress! And

> you can see even on this committee, how many of us are teachers. So our teachers not only back the campaign, they are central to it, they see it as integral to their job as teachers – to support and prepare the young instructors, and to coordinate the campaign wherever they work. They are proud to accompany their students to the villages and work with them. They are always ready. They know their responsibilities and tasks.[1]

Dereje Bekkele also emphasised that the Ethiopian Trade Union Association (AETU) had a direct and very important part to play in the campaign. In Sidamo, the trade unions were active in flour processing, and also in the state farms, gold mining and lumber camps. They mobilised their entire membership — with 'those who were literate teaching, and those who were illiterate learning'. And if trade union members went to the rural areas from the cities to teach, then employers — whether state or private — were expected to continue to pay the workers' salaries. Trade unions also had an important fund–raising function. Through dramatic productions, bazaars, football matches and cultural events they raised large sums of money which were paid into the campaign's national account. As Dereje Bekkele spoke of these efforts, I thought of our own children and teachers in Sheffield, raising money and support in very much the same way. As I told the regional committee of their work and achievements, and showed photographs of Sheffield children and their teachers and parents marching across the English city one frozen Sunday morning, with their placards declaring 'Pencils for Ethiopia', there was a warmth in the room strong enough to cross continents.

The Work of one Kebele

Close to the shore of Lake Awassa is the neighbourhood of Awassa city represented by Higher 2 Kebele – 6. While I visited the literacy centre in this Kebele, housed in the primary school, its president handed me a copy of the latest report, or as he referred to it, 'a bird's–eye view of its literacy work'. It indicates, very clearly, the Ethiopian achievement in miniature, in one specific suburb in a regional city. The report was prepared in English:

> As you all know, in the transformation of society, education becomes a part of the comprehensive revolution in ideology and culture, without which the old social order cannot be finally overcome. That being that: this campaign had been launched ten years ago. Since then we had 19 educational campaign rounds. In each round we had an average number of 41 illiterate participants. Out of these, 571 were female and 217

were male. This Kebele has a population of 3,131 people in number.

Undergoing the 19 rounds of the campaign we have let 126 students to regular schools around. To execute this campaign in our Kebele we have been assisted by materials from the National Literacy Campaign Coordinating Committee. To cite a few, the Urban Dwellers Literacy Campaign Coordinating Committee of our Kebele has received so far:
80 dozens of pencils,152 gross chalk and about 2,500 different students books.

The Kebele Campaign Coordinating Committee in its own educational organisation system has four different committees. These are:

(i) Educational materials procurement and distribution committee

(ii) Recruitment, training and placement committee

(iii) Propaganda and aid coordinating committee

(iv) Data collection, supervision and certificate organising committee

The number of teachers who participated in this campaign is 143, out of which regular teachers selected out of the literate living people of the Kebele are 56, whereas student–teachers who participated through the educational campaign are 97. We feel very happy when the youth teach their fathers and mothers.

The execution of this campaign had some problems, though not major. But all were overcome by the hard and united action of the coordinating committee, being assisted by the urban dwellers association of the Kebele.

In addition to those, we are contributing funds for such areas as Arero and Borena sub–provinces, which are unable to run the campaign by themselves, and we do this through the regional administrative office.[2]

In a post–literacy class in the Kebele centre I spoke to several of the students, who had recently become literate as a result of the nineteenth round, and who were now consolidating that achievement in the twentieth. One of these was Tsegaye Beyene, a 66 year old ex–policeman, now a pensioner. He had joined the police force in 1941, but during the next three decades, working under the imperial regime, he had received no help in his wish to become literate.

All my life I wanted to know how read and write. Then I could have done my job better and had a chance of promotion. I had to beg to write, somebody else had to do it for me. My daughter went to India to become a teacher. I could never write to her, and if she wrote to me I had to run around to find someone to read the letter.

Now I can read and I can write too. I want to spend the rest of my life usefully, and read everything I could never know about before. Education doesn't stop with age, you know. In Ethiopia, often it only begins for us then. And it makes us feel that we can start up new work, start everything again in our lives. As for me, I want to be able to do anything which my country needs me for.[3]

'The Grass Itself Speaking'

One hundred and sixty–five kilometres on from Awassa is the town of Sodo, the centre of the Awraja of Wollaita. It is a very densely populated province with 1,100,000 people — over 250 every square kilometre. Cool and undulating, the land rises from 950 to 3,500 metres, covered with small farms concentrating upon cattle, coffee and root crops. Over the last few years, with the electrification of the province, some 167 new villages have been established under the government's villagisation programme, with a total population of 135,176.

But the Awraja is particularly proud of its progress in education. I was to begin to understand the meaning of the slogan 'Fill the environment with letters' in the villages of Sodo–Wollaita, but before that I had the opportunity to take note of the logistics of the campaign. The primary spur to motivate literacy recruitment – the growth of elementary schools for the peasants' own children – had reached 189 new schools, with four secondary schools. 93,687 students were now attending, being taught by 1,875 teachers. The development of a nursery system was a particular feature of the Awraja, and 17 new kindergartens had been established in some of the villages, staffed by 26 nursery teachers.

As Gebre Michael Challa, the Awraja administrator, told me about the history of the campaign in Sodo–Wollaita, a sense of cultural pride seemed to radiate from him. Later in the day I was to see why. What struck me as he spoke was that although the expression of the campaign's objectives in each new location that I visited carried a consistent underlying similarity, the emphases were very often different, as if they had been measured against local conditions and priorities, and the political consciousness of their formulators. For example, here in Wollaita, the three main objectives put forward were:

(i) To provide the political armament of the awareness of our revolution.

(ii) To establish progressive socialist culture.

(iii) To eliminate undesirable cultural elements which can hinder our development.[4]

It was also becoming clearer and clearer to me, as the administration pointed to graphs, charts, statistical tables which filled the walls of his office, and an incredibly detailed map of the region showing the location of literacy centres wereda by wereda and village by village, how important data collection and the exactitude of a statistical base were to those organising the campaign.

The concrete result of this information was that the campaign had produced 651,202 newly–literate people since it began, considerably more than half of the entire population of the Awraja. To service these graduates and to ensure their retention of literacy skills, 177 reading centres had been opened, and a local newspaper published regularly in Wolayitigna, the main local language, called *Bakalia* ('Morning Star') and another, *Nigat* ('Dawn') in Amharic. 58 new listening centres had been provided with radios – which had also been given out as prizes by the Awraja coordinating committee to the most successful centres. Another emphasis in Gebre Michael Challa's summary of the campaign was the work–oriented literacy links with cottage industry projects in the villages, like metalworking, carpentry, crocheting, tanning, ceramics and weaving.

When Dawit Shumbulo, the administrator of the Wereda of Damotgalle, — where the villages I was to visit were situated — spoke of the pedagogy of the literacy centres which were his responsibility 'turning education into play', I was curious. For these were adults who were learning, so what did he mean? As he told me about the methods of improvisation the teachers had employed, falling back totally on their own resources and the natural and existing materials in and around the villages themselves, I had little idea of what I would find. 'We shall always find a way, whatever happens', he declared, as he told me about the local dyes they used to paint blackboards, the moist red soil which served as ink, the grass itself speaking. The grass itself speaking! What was going on here? What was he saying, as he smiled at me, almost mischievously?

The Awraja coordinating commitee members were particularly proud of the contribution of local people to the campaign. For although essential items such as chalk, blackboard, books and uniforms and blankets for the campaigners were supplied by the National Literacy Campaign Coordinating Committee, everything else was provided by contributions from local people. Sometimes if the campaign's supplies were delayed or exhausted, expedients had to be found – like extracting lumps of chalk from locally–found calcium deposits. But local fund–raising had realised 77,869 Birr (approximately $40,000 US), and this had enabled valuable 'extras' to be bought, like a camera, radios and a duplicating machine. In addition the people had paid for and constructed shelters, classrooms, reading rooms, listening centres and food for the campaigners. So much so, as Dawit Shumbulo affirmed: 'This is truly the people's campaign, for without these contributions, the aims of the programme would never have been fulfilled'.

Early Morning in Boditi

Boditi is the small town at the centre of the Wereda of Damotgalle. From around six in the morning the literacy students arrive for their classes, which have to finish by just before eight o'clock when the school day for the primary school children begins. They share the same classrooms. In one class the young woman teacher is energetically raising and dropping flash cards as the students shout back the correct word: 'kettle', 'calf', 'cucumber', 'soldier', 'bread' or 'sisal'. Next door a basic Maths class is in progress. The twelfth grade teacher has rigged up an improvised abacus which looks something like a clothes horse, with the different numbers suspended on wires held between two small posts. As he changes around the numbers to create different sums, students come out to the blackboard and write their answers. The blackboard is democratised and is clearly not seen as the property of the teacher! Another class is at the post literacy level, and a group of mostly mature men are practising sentence–building, all on the theme of water, 'There is no life without water', one writes in Amharic: 'Plants cannot exist without water', writes another.

As this lesson draws to a close, the general movement and sounds of many voices outside mean the familiar bustle of children gathering for a morning assembly. There are hundreds of young people, many holding hoes and small forks for their work on the land later in the day, and all with an armful of books. As they form up in their years to sing the National Anthem and hear the daily notices from the school director, the impact of the formal education of thousands of Ethiopian children on the lives and education of adults becomes more and more evident. It is their parents who were in their classrooms before them, learning letters, sentences and numbers, and their own parents whose urge to learn has been propelled forward by their own children's educational progress. As the huge sound of hundreds of children singing their country's anthem resounds around the school, the same parents emerge from the common classrooms.

As I am walking back from the school with Dawit Shumbulo, a young man runs up to me, waving a letter. Dawit translates his eager words. His name is Doda Dolla, he says, and he wants to show me his first letter! This is the first complete piece of writing he has ever written, he says, his face a landscape of smiles. Dated 6/2/81 in the Ethiopian calendar, the letter is written to his brother in another Awraja:

> Dear Brother Gasso Dolla
>
> How are you? I am very well and also our family are all well too.
>
> Besides giving you this greeting, I want to show you that I can now read and write! So now I can read books, and look, I can also write a letter like this to you. It's a letter of celebration, and I write it with great happiness.
>
> Please give my greetings to your family.
>
> Ethiopia First!
>
> Doda Dolla

'Fill the Environment with Letters!'

As the Land Rover I was travelling in with a group of representatives from the Adult Education Department from Addis Ababa pulled towards Ade Offa village, it was met by a group of men mounted on their small galloping horses, brandishing their literacy primers and singing out slogans. As they reined in their horses, the bells on their metal harnesses tinkled and the rays of the sun striped their embroidered saddle cloths, lighting up the lion designs and the multi–coloured patterns. They chanted together in Wolayitigna, 'Our revolution has brought us into the light' and 'Our literacy campaign is a part of our cultural revolution'. As the jeep moved slowly, escorted by the horsemen, towards the giant wooden arch which made the entrance to the village, everything around seemed to have labels and notices nailed upon them – trees,

Above: A twelfth grade campaigner in Boditi.
Below: The 'grass speaking' in Ade Offa village:

horses, plots of land, objects. Through the arch was a large bed of earth where carved–out turfs formed the shapes of letters, numbers and words. So this was the grass speaking! 'Let's read! Let's write! Let's learn! We shall eradicate illiteracy' was written across the soil of Ade Offa village. And between the houses, along the pathways, all the way to the literacy centre etched in turf were maps of Africa, of Ethiopia with the boundaries of its 14 regions clearly marked, of Sidamo Region, Wollaita Awraja and Damotgalle Wereda. Damit Shumbulo proudly pointed to all these grass drawings, stepping over continents, regions, lakes and provinces as he did so.

To enter the literacy sub–centre we went through a revolving wooden bamboo door. Once through, this was not so much a literacy centre as a literacy village in itself, an entire environment of language. Letters were everywhere: over the earth, on the walls of houses, on large pictures and figures painted onto banged–out pieces of corrugated iron erected every few yards, with bubbles of words spewing out from the mouths of painted literacy campaigners and students. People walked around the village quite naturally with labels affixed to their shoulders, arms and chests: 'tanner', 'ironsmith', 'weaver', 'potter'. Everywhere you looked you focussed upon a Wolayitigna word – even the sky, crossed with the huge wooden arch crowded with messages and slogans.

The building which housed the literacy class, made of brown, dried earth bricks, was festooned across its outside walls with letters to be used as flashcards, cut from cardboard, corrugated iron and pieces of polystyrene and painted in bright colours. In the classroom itself, a young twelfth grade campaigner called Bergane Banti was teaching a post–literacy class who were in the process of making the transition from their mother tongue, Wolayitigna, to Amharic. Oshene Alambo, a young farmer, spoke profusely about what he felt he had gained from the campaign:

> First, I think I have impoved myself. Now I am free of illiteracy there is so much I can gain from reading. As I sit and read in our reading room I learn about new ways of farming, ways that are much more modern and give me more yield.
>
> Now I am conserving my soil better because I understand the effects of deforestation on my land and why these terrible cracks come across our earth. So I've stopped destroying trees, I'm now planting them instead. And I have started alternate farming – I leave some of my land fallow every year.

Now I am writing letters to my family in Shashamene and Awassa — before someone else did it for me. I can't exactly forecast how being able to read and write will bring me more money, but I know it will improve my situation. But more than anything I feel as if I am myself at last.[5]

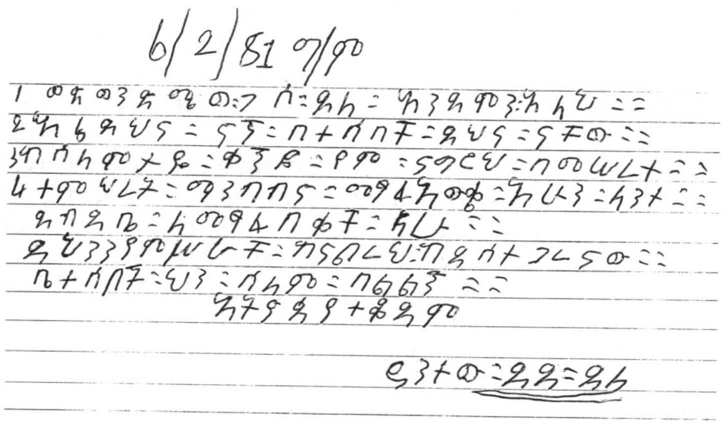

Above: Doda Dolla's first letter.
Below: Mekonnen Debissa and his 'teaching target'.

'Let Everything be Used!'

Immediately outside the literacy class, the innovations that Oshene Alambo had spoken of were being demonstrated, directly relating the word to the world, and letters to betterment. A model of a new village had been constructed, intended to serve as an example in the parallel processes of literacy and villagisation. Miniature houses had been built in rows, each of them separated off into rooms for kitchen, general living, storage and animal stables. Along the street between the houses, dried gourds painted red and yellow hung on twine, representing electrification, and bamboo stems half–buried between the houses indicated the coming of pipe–borne water. There was also a model well, clinic and school/literacy centre, and these small buildings were just large enough for people to enter at a stoop, and sit and discuss the developments right outside of their literacy or post–literacy class. Between the centre and the row of houses sheltering cottage industries, where labelled craftsmen and craftswomen tanned leather, spun cotton thread, made baskets, wove cloth, pumped goatskin bellows and hammered tools and utensils – was a spectacular and ornate map of Africa in pale blue flowers, the nations marked out by carefully hoed borders. Large banged–out iron plates every few yards displayed Wolayitigna syllabary and a car wheel and iron rod hung ready to summon students to the next class. I remembered Neway Wolde Sadik telling me in Addis Ababa that in the villages 'nothing is left unused'.

In the Literacy Campaign office, not one square inch of wall was left uncovered. Charts, tables, evaluation reports and graphs were all over the wall like wallpaper! Ethiopia is nurturing a nation of statisticians in these villages. Nothing is left casually suspended in guesswork or inexactitude. Every single advance is noted, every number calculated, every problem set down. Against the names of student teachers were records of what they had taught and covered in every single class, work plans were displayed for every round of the campaign and the shelves were full of home–made files detailing all aspects of the campaign's work. This was a factor I found consistently everywhere I went in Sidamo — records, evaluations, precise details, exact numbers, specific reports. It was a demonstration to all involved of the uses of numeracy, a continuous exemplar of a scientific approach to development. Halfway up one wall were the words of the *International*, set down in Wolayitigna. As Dawit Shumbulo started singing them softly, it was the one–world chorus that I could join in with, in my own language.

In the reading room next to the office, teaching aids, flash cards and cut–out letters hung everywhere from walls, windows, wooden beams and pillars like Christmas streamers and decorations. I had to dodge and weave to avoid the bashed–out tin can letters and cardboard numbers that seemed to be flying around the room, over the heads of the dozen or so readers. Under the window a young teacher stood next to his own invention made from flattened corrugated iron into three concentric circles fixed together so each revolved inside the other. They were brightly painted with syllables on their outside, and when turned would make words and short sentences through different combinations. The students would then be asked to read these from this 'target' look–alike device. Words and sentences had been made from dried beads and berries stuck to cardboard; ceramic syllables had been formed and baked from the red earth outside the village houses, a silk–screen frame had been made from wooden struts, locally produced dyes, with a heavy bottle used as a roller. There was a home–made megaphone formed from corrugated iron, a cardboard television set with sums appearing from a paper scroll which was reeled up from below by handles attached to a bamboo pole.

Outside the reading room a man was struggling with a plough being pulled by a single donkey across a small plot of land. This was a demonstration of the ploughing innovation, using a donkey rather than two oxen, that Abdela Sonessa, the President of EPA had told me about. As the literacy students beheld this, they also saw demonstrations of new bee–keeping techniques in hives behind the reading room, which they reached by stepping through a small bed of rows of medicinal herbs, including the all–purpose Katikala plant, which was mixed with meat, coffee and local alcoholic drinks to make a remedy for colds, malaria, influenza and headaches. Further on was a full–size model farmhouse, constructed, as everything else in this 'literacy village' had been, by the joint work of local people and campaigners, mobilized by the village peasants association. Literacy and post literacy students were wandering in and out of the house, noting the arrangement of rooms, the different storage compartments and the positions of the animal stalls. Around the side of its walls was a creche area for the children of those in study, with a childminder organising games for infants, and older children playing on wooden swings and leaping and balancing across a set of village–made parallel bars. For the elderly there was a leisure area, and a group of older men were busy with an energetic game of Gebetta, launching their stones into the various cavities of a carved wooden board. Next to their house of recreation was a ziggurat–shaped structure of mud bricks, with labels showing the huge 1979 national percentage of illiterates at the bottom, gradually tapering towards the much smaller plateau at the top, as the percentage decreased towards 1988.

This was a lot to take in. So much made out of so little in the way of what teachers in Europe might see as 'available resources'. Yet the genius behind this popular pedagogy had created an integration between the world of learning and the real world that was absolutely total. It was true, everything was being used for the purposes of teaching and learning, and for demonstrating the way forward towards economic and social development.

On to Ade Aro

As you drive into the next village called Ade Aro, past the fields of maize, the plots of bananas, the pastures full of cattle, the reservoir stopped up by an earthen dam and a well–grassed and levelled football pitch, there is a large painting of a child on a flattened section of corrugated iron which proclaims in Wolayitigna: 'Children need love and peace'. In the village itself a group of women are breaking tradition by building a house, moulding the bricks with the moist brown earth next to the walls which they are raising. All through the village there are the same words, letters, sentences, and maps written and drawn in the turf, and also shaped in gathered stones.

Inside the reading room, Lencha Data, a 50 year old farmer, is reading a local newspaper. He looks up and tells the colleague with me how much he has learned about his own country and its events since he became literate, and how much more sense he can make of the Wolayitigna and national radio programmes. He also talks enthusiastically about his farming and how it has improved, now he can read: 'Before I wasn't systematic. For instance, I used to scatter my seeds when I sowed. Now I sow in rows and use the fertilisers we are given by the government.' Also there is Mekonnen Debissa, the young teacher from Ade Offa, who has come with us to this village. He tells us he is a full–time teacher in a neighbouring village, but does voluntary literacy tasks in Ade Offa and Ade Aro, along with the rest of the team of ten campaigners who are assigned here. 'It was all group activity that made these literacy villages', he explains. 'We creatively applied the directives of the regional Co-ordinating Committee, and came up with our own ideas here, all made with whatever resources and materials we could find locally.

Members of other neighbouring village committees come to see our work – and they imitate and apply it in their own contexts. Sometimes they come openly, sometimes they come 'underground' and spy us out! They want to be the best centre and get the emulation award! But this means that all our people benefit, and each village is encouraged to be more and more inventive and resourceful in the way that it applies its own original ideas to the development of the literacy campaign'.

Farmers of Ade Aro village.

'If the Drought Comes Again'

As we left Ade Aro, it became clear to me that young teachers like Mekonnen Debissa were the sap of this campaign which had so many millions of heroes. They were the teachers, the source of dedication and permanent creativity. Through their innovations, their round–the–clock inventiveness and their ability to apply their pedagogy using everything in the real world around them, they had motivated mass learning and made education come alive for millions of Ethiopians.

Back in Boditi, I had the opportunity to have a final discussion with Dawit Shumbulo and his colleagues of the Wereda Coordinating Committee. He explained how important the campaign had been for institutionalising the process of villagisation. The new schools and the campaign, along with the three new clinics, the four pharmacies and the ten first–aid centres had been the vital catalysts for compacting the people. In terms of figures, out of the Wereda's total population of 236,869, 71% of the people were now literate – which almost exactly parallelled the national figures of 1987 of 70.8%. Yet what the committee members were most satisfied about was its orientation. They had succeeded in relating it intimately to the world of work and the need for better health. The Wereda approach was firmly to create Work–oriented literacy and Diet–oriented literacy. This had leapt into the consciousness of the students — learn to read and write and you will work better, enjoy better yields from your land and also you and your family will be more healthy. This had proved to be a source of genuine and high motivation for the people of the local villages. It had made the campaign itself the main motor of their economic development and concretely changed their lives. As Dawit Shumbulo concluded: 'The campaign has definitely been the main vehicle promoting the gains of the revolution. We have seen a dual flow of development. The Ministry of Agriculture, for example, provides us with fertiliser and high quality seeds. But it is the literacy campaign that has taught the correct use of these resources through its texts and work–orientation. We have also felt much more a part of our country and its wholeness through the campaign. We're not just little villages in a distant Wereda anymore. We are a part of Ethiopia – we are Ethiopia and the campaign has given us a constant togetherness with the rest of our country. It has made a distinct difference for the better'.

Much of Sodo–Wollaita, including this Wereda, had been badly afflicted by the disastrous drought of 1984–5. So remembering the word 'armament' they had used when describing the objectives of the literacy campaign, I asked the colleagues what kind of 'armament' had the campaign given them to withstand the effect of any climatic disaster of the future? What if a drought came again, or, as had also happened in the past, there had been a damaging over–abundance of rain? 'Our literacy campaign, more than anything else', they affirmed , 'has taught us how education and life, and the theory and practice of both can never be separated. Through our campaign we have conserved our soil, fought back against erosion, learned to more efficiently store our water in the artificial pools which we have constructed'. And Dawit Shumbulo interjected, 'And do you know that during the last decade, since the campaign started, we have learned and practised the lessons of re–forestation? We have planted five million seedlings, just in our Wereda. For words are no use just by themselves sitting on the pages of books. It is how we use them, and build our new life in Ethiopia with them that really matters'.

Notes

1. From discussion with Sidamo Regional Co-ordinating Committee, Awassa, October 1988.
2. From report of Higher 2 *Kebele* 6, Awassa, on the progress of the National Literacy Campaign in the Region, October 1988.
3. Interview with Tsegaye Beyene, Awassa, October 1988.
4. 'The Development of the Literacy Campaign in Wollaita *Awraja*', Report:
5. Interview with Oshene Alambo, Ade Offa, Sidamo, October 1988.

Potter in Ade Aro village with her 'label'.

8.
LITERACY, AND AFTER

These teachers and learners of Sodo–Wollaita in Sidamo region were a part of a people, remember, who 'won't do anything for themselves', as Rupert Murdoch's *Sun* blazed across its editorial one British weekday morning in 1986. In fact between 1979 and 1988, some twenty–one million illiterate Ethiopians had taken part in their National Literacy Campaign, and 18.7 million of these had successfully learned the skills of reading and writing. This achievement, combined with the progress made through the much–expanded formal school system, had resulted in a 1988 literacy figure of 75.3%. And the higher proportion of these graduates of literacy centres all over Ethiopia (51.8%), have been the long–oppressed Ethiopian women. As to their teachers, 1,788,000 literacy instructors taught in the first 17 rounds, more than the entire literate population of Ethiopia before the 1974 Revolution.

Thus, when a peasant speaks of his former reluctance to take his cattle to the veterinary department because he feared that the vet would steal them, but now says how the local Health Officer has given him books which enable him to read about the benefits of vaccination for his animals: it is the literacy campaign which is the cause.[1] When a tailor tells how only a year or so ago he would measure his cloth using his fingers and arms and thus make inaccurate cuts and dissatisfied customers, but now he uses a tape measure and cuts his cloth exactly: it is because of the literacy campaign. When there is a general raising of efficiency all over the country in the managing of household budgets: again it is the effect of the literacy campaign. When the most popular and respected candidates elected to positions of responsibility in the mass organisations of the women, youth, peasantry, workers and town dwellers are predominantly those who have successfully passed through the literacy campaign – then its impact is permanently evidenced. For it has been a central factor in moving Ethiopian society and its economy away from the backwardness of its very recent feudal past, and the low level of economic and social development which characterised it, towards new forms of socialisation and production. It has helped to create the possibility of a modern state, with a people prepared to understand and use the necessary science and technology.

This has been achieved using a system that is brilliantly simple: the replication of the broad, cross–social and cross–ministerial National Literacy Campaign Coordinating Committee at every level of the campaign's activity — from the national level to the village level. Thus all that is necessary to achieve — from recruitment to text distribution to data collection to certification — is achieved by a standing structure down to the most local level. Take the mechanisms for evaluation and monitoring, for example. The Coordinating Committee, whether at national, regional, Awraja, Wereda, Kebele or village level can send a monitoring or evaluation team (made up of representatives from the sub–committee of Data Collection, Supervision and Certification) to representative sample centres to assess progress in the campaign through interviewing, observation and checklisting.[2] The structure is there at every level to utilise, and it is so fundamentally simple as to be able to protect itself from bureaucratisation. Its development has been organically Ethiopian and has arisen directly from the unique democratic organisations that sprouted from the mass, popular activity of the Ethiopian Revolution.

What is the response of the people who studied, those who have graduated through this epic educational project? In 1984, in a pamphlet, the National Literacy Campaign Coordinating Committee published a list of responses made to journalists and interviewers, by those who had recently passed through the campaign. These tell the story of a people whose lives have been transformed in those details and moments that make up life itself, and read like a living collective poem:

'I no longer have to ask people the number of the bus I have to take'

'No longer do I have to ask my son to read letters to me'
'Now I feel that I am a real person, and I will be happy to die'
'Using the telephone now is no problem. I can read the numbers'
'When I draw my salary I sign my name proudly with the others'
'Now I can write to my friends in other regions, and I can read their letters when they write to me'

'It is now possible to read the newspaper and find out what is happening in different parts of the country. Before, I could only look at the pictures'
'I am going to continue my studies. I am going to learn more about electricity''
'I am more than 80 years old.People said I was too old to learn but why should I not be able to read and write with the others?'
'Now I can read the notices in our cooperative, and we are all able to work better'
'Now I can read the receipt from the taxes I paid and the farming instructions given by the extension worker'[3]

No relapse!
A village reading room.

Struggling Against Relapse

A worker in the Ministry of Education in Addis Ababa, Fantaye Worku, has written a strong poem about the measures needed to be taken to ensure the retention of literacy among those millions of Ethiopians who are graduates of the campaign.

No Relapse!

Even though it may seem that illiteracy has been wiped away
Although it seems that its fortress has been destroyed,
When we forget what it stands for
It only revives!

We have to understand that it is our number one enemy
'No relapse into illiteracy!'
This is the call of our times.

So let us strengthen our unity
Let us fortify our struggle against illiteracy
Let us start from a knowledge of our society
Let us make education full of life
To spread newspapers out to the villages –

It is the time to multiply our reading rooms
Let us give our full attention to them,
They are our guarantee to keep up our people's literacy
They are like rivers which will never run dry.

When we educate people
And make new readers,
We must also remember
Never to let them relapse.
For even though an illiterate people may seem to be alive
In reality they are dead!
So let us bring knowledge to our people,
To those who are living in the dark.

Of course, once a people achieve literacy, the stuggle continues to sustain it. 'Every Ethiopian will be literate and remain literate!' declares the slogan. This process of consolidation of words in the context of Ethiopia, again requires a massive effort of mobilisation and popular will. At the time of writing (November 1988) some 13.6 million Ethiopians are involved in post–literacy classes of two hours daily study for five days a week. They are studying Mathematics, Health Education, Family Education and Environmental Science, and while doing so millions are making the transition from their first language of nationality to Amharic. Already over fifty million books, mainly functional readers, have been printed and distributed to the post–literacy students on such specific life–related curriculum themes as Cooperative Education, Political Education, First Aid, Pest Control, Soil Conservation, Coffee Planting and Remedying Traditional Malpractice. In order to stimulate local newspaper–making, quarterly newspapers have been produced for the post–literacy effort in five languages, with 144,300 copies of each of the 21 issues already having reached the students. The publications, together with those produced at regional, district, village or Kebele level, are displayed in the 7,900 reading rooms that have been constructed and equipped in literacy centres throughout the nation. These mini–libraries have also become the listening venues where the newly–literate students come to listen to the radio lessons regularly transmitted by the Ministry of Education in order to support and supplement the topics dealt within the post–literacy functional readers. The reading rooms themselves are reinforced at roadside sites, in village centres or places of community activity, by the reading stalls, where people can stand and read local and national newspapers, notices of local interest and concern and extracts from the functional readers themselves.

All this learning activity has made reading a part of the daily rhythm of Ethiopian life in its villages and urban neighbourhoods. The book is now a friend and the word a tool, and it is in this entirely new context that other post–literacy strategies of adult education have been established. For the literacy campaign has been pivotal for any progress in this sector. It has been, in the words of Mammo Kebbede Shenkut, 'the doorway to adult education'.

Strategies for Post–literacy

With the vast majority of Ethiopians living in rural areas, an important initiative, stretching back to the pre–literacy campaign days of the mid–seventies, has been the nationwide establishing of 408 Community Skills Training Centres. These seek to upgrade and develop the skills that the people already have, in the context of appropriate technologies and creative innovations. Short, four month courses are offered on traditional skills like tanning, beekeeping, basketry, animal husbandry and weaving, and also training is given to paraprofessionals like midwives and health workers. Emphasis is placed particularly in these courses upon self–reliance and self–

sufficiency, while also stressing the strongest of respect for understanding and conserving the richness and provision of the natural environment. These items are also to the fore in the Basic Development Education Programme, which trains and encourages rural communities to fully maximise their own local and natural resources — something which has been so important for the success of the people's pedagogy in the literacy campaign. The pioneering basic technology centre at Burayu has made a substantial contribution to this programme which is designed to offer creative and inventive local solutions to chronic rural problems. For example, it is pointless simply to tell a peasant who is dependent on wood for his fuel: 'Don't cut wood, you're destroying the forests and ruining your soil'. An alternative has to be offered. So the Basic Education Development Programme has developed a wood–saving stove which has a very low wood consumption, with one kilo serving as fuel for two or three days. Likewise, wood is being conserved through the construction of houses and furniture using mud blocks, and the development of solar cookers.[4]

Another strategy which has grown in importance as the literacy campaign has reached more and more people is the Distance Education programme. This was originally conceived as a method of reaching post–literacy students through radio in isolated communities in the countryside, but its courses have become particularly important as in–service opportunities for Ethiopia's 17,000 unqualified primary school teachers, particularly those in remote areas who are unable to follow regular in–college courses. 40% of the Distance Education students are teachers at this level, and another 26% are soldiers, with rural health and government workers, housewives and transport workers also widely involved. There are plans to make Distance Education a vehicle for large numbers of the newly–literate, as it could be an efficient as well as cost–effective strategy for such students (as it has proved in Tanzania). But the most popular and widely–subscribed system of continuing education for adults in Ethiopia is still Night School, even though the students at the present time follow the same courses and general curriculum as their children during the day. With 47.8% of night school adults following a primary school syllabus, 12.2% a junior secondary and 37% a senior secondary syllabus, there remains an obvious need to re–make a curriculum much more suitable for the needs of adults and geared to the difficulties they face and the development and production priorities which they identify.

A Literate Environment

As the villages in Sodo–Wollaita are demonstrating with such originality, an imperative for a nation of neo–literates is the creation of a literate environment, where everywhere you turn, everywhere you look, from the earth to the sky and everything in between – there are letters and numbers. To transform surroundings which never knew or expressed the written word into a living book — that is the achievement of villages like Ade Aro and Ade Offa, and thousands of other rural centres all over Ethiopia. Such villages also model the marriage of literacy and development. For primarily, a people need to *understand* the need for progress, and it is through the word that this conscientisation grows. With such an understanding, the skills which are learned through the tools of literacy then directly develop and progress the living conditions, earning potential and economic development of the people and their society. This in turn creates new wealth, and more jobs and salaries. And at the centre of this process is mass education and the literacy campaign.

When Yohannes Beraki, the young director of Misrak Comprehensive High School in Addis Ababa told me that during three shifts every day 5,790 people use his school – which was meant to accommodate a few hundred — he declared: 'that is the result of our literacy campaign! Our people believe in learning, believe in language. We are all teaching each other and learning from each other. Without the campaign this could not have happened!' When Doda Dolla of Boditi came running at me breathless with his first letter, the message of happiness to his brother which proclaimed his literacy and entry into the reading world, the world of words and communications, he spoke like a man seizing a new life. He had created his first ever complete piece of writing, he had given birth, like millions of other Ethiopians, to a personal, living literature. It is the same literature displayed on reading booths, where men tie up their horses and women put down their baskets in order to stop and read the rural newsletters which their neighbours, now journalists, have composed. And from this literature they discuss, they create ideas and find solutions to their problems in the most practical life–surviving and life–enchancing ways. Each of these wooden reading stalls, every reading room, every syllable of earth baked in the sun, every turfed letter, every young twelfth grade campaigner, every elderly learner emerging from serfdom through letters, every woman student throwing off the drudgery of generations means a victory for Ethiopia in the epic battle it is fighting against such a formidable enemy. As Neway Wolde Sadik expressed this struggle with such a determined waging of words:

> ...what a huge arch–enemy to all humanity is illiteracy! Illiteracy ranks alongside ignorance, disease and poverty as a terrible source of underdevelopment to people everywhere. So we have declared war upon it![5]

Notes

1. See film by UNESCO, 1985: *The Battle for Literacy.*
2. Mammo Kebbede Shenkut: *Summary Report of a Meeting on the development of techniques and procedures of evaluation and monitoring pertaining to programmes of literacy, post–literacy and Continuing Education in the framework of Lifelong Education*, Hamburg, April 1988.
3. *Every Ethiopian will be literate and remain literate*, National Literacy Campaign Coordinating Committee, Addis Ababa, 1984.
4. See *Government Roles in the Ethiopian Adult Education*, Mammo Kebbede Shenkut, Sydney, 1988.
5. Wolde Sadik/Searle *At the Gateway of Light*, Sheffield, 1986.

No relapse!
A roadside reading booth.